I0620656

# High on Life Not on Stuff:

How to Stop Buying Things You Don't Need

Evgenia Stroganova

By a regular woman and work in progress who hopes to help you save yourself time and money, obtain more joy and freedom, understand yourself more deeply, and not get consumed by consumption.

*How long does your shopping usually last? These days mine is normally twenty to forty minutes. If I am lucky enough, it only takes me about twenty minutes to see what I need, try it, and buy it. Done. Sometimes, it has to take longer, but once I get that specific thing I need, I am out. With a light heart, I am walking out of the store, away from the exhausting trap of consumption, toward life, towards-everything I love that I can do using the time and money I save. To me, shopping has a utilitarian nature and is not a hobby – except for occasions when I'm purchasing something for a new beginning, such as a painting kit when I am learning how to paint, a book I am excited to read, or other things that are related to activities. My friends stopped inviting me for shopping trips on weekends, as unless we were looking for something specific, I would most likely opt out. I do not consider regular shopping a type of entertainment or rest; it tires me and drives me crazy when it takes too long and does not have a specific purpose. The same applies to online shopping. It was not always this way. This positive change in my life has been happening thanks to a certain amount of self-awareness, analysis, brainstorming, and experimenting, and I would like to share my humble thoughts and experiences with you in the hope that you may find these useful may also share some of yours and we can build some consumerism resistance together.*

# About the Author

Evgenia Stroganova is a passionate lifelong learner with a deep love for self-development and creativity. She holds a Master of Arts in Asian Studies, a diploma in video game design and animation, and speaks four languages. With a Russian and Ukrainian background, she grew up in Russia, studied in China and moved to Canada in 2009, where she now resides with her growing family.

Writing has been a part of Evgenia's life since childhood. She began with fairy tales for her younger brother and an endearingly simplistic "book about the world" before expanding into poetry and translations of modern Chinese verse. It was in Canada that her love for learning and self-improvement intertwined with her passion for writing.

Through self-reflection, research, and humor, Evgenia crafted this book to address the pervasive issue of excessive consumerism.

# Contents

# How And Why This Book Was Written

---

In 2014, on a sunny spring day, I was sitting on the floor of my room, not knowing where to begin packing. You never realize how many belongings you have until you need to pack them all up to move to a new place. And when you do, you feel surprised and overwhelmed; well, at least I did, and this unpleasant feeling made me procrastinate. I had put my packing off until the last moment and was now sitting on the floor, encouraging myself to begin. Earlier that day, I listened to music, browsed the internet, and practiced some salsa dance moves I'd recently learned. In short, I was doing everything but packing as if I was secretly and shamefully afraid of and was hiding from, like a child trying to hide from unwanted homework.

I was surprised by how much stuff I had. I thought, *really?* Could I not see that if I was buying much, I would have a lot? I laughed to myself or you can say at myself. It feels surreal, and it hit me hard. I was shocked to see that I had so many things that were too similar. To give you a context of what I am talking about, I had 5 pairs of scissors. In my thought process, I was stuck on why I had so many scissors. Given that, the pair of scissors I used was already in my kitchen. I felt something different; I felt something was not right; maybe there was a problem.

It didn't feel like I had that much stuff; in fact, at times, it felt like I didn't have enough. Then what were all these items watching me from the table, shelves, bookcase, closet, and drawers? Not to mention the kitchen— I love to eat, and I love cooking and baking. And it seemed like I stored enough food to survive another week or two, as if there was a zombie invasion coming, and I had to lock myself in my apartment and survive. The washroom was similarly crowded; as a modern woman in Canada, I 'had to' have an extensive collection of creams, skincare, and makeup products, different types of shampoo, and many other things. Or maybe this idea has been pushed upon us by advertisements and social media. Maybe some societal norms are the biggest dilemmas, or you can say scams. They will trap you in an unnoticed manner. They will seep into you very slowly and steadily and create their spaces in the subconscious mind.

It was a day full of discoveries; I greeted many items I did not even remember I had. And why would I if, once I got them, I put them in the back of my closet behind all that mess? I honestly was ashamed of myself. I felt like I had done something wrong; I shouldn't have done that; I shouldn't have bought all those unnecessary things I don't even need in my life.

I told my roommate - let's call her D - that I would be ready with my packing in four hours, but it took me until the next morning, and when she woke up, I was still running around, my hair as messy as my state of mind. It felt like I was battling with all the stuff I had and kept discovering, and I was not winning the battle. She laughed at me, and so did I.

We are good friends, and we still laugh about it today. Since then, when I tell her how long I am planning to spend on packing, she says we should multiply it by three or four to get the actual time needed. And, to be fair, we all know that packing always tends to take longer than expected, doesn't it?

Soon after this, I was moving – yet again! – to another place and do it urgently. I barely had time to pack as I was escaping from some unexpected mess that I'd inadvertently created in my life. Left without proper boxes and containers, I had to pack half of my things into plastic bags of all sizes. The scenery created was rather comical and made my friends who came to help me giggle. I was giggling, too, giggling and blushing, blushing and giggling. The comical component was interfering with the sense of embarrassment and they were competing with each other in my poor head. Anyone who was coming to my place was laughing out loud. I felt bad. I just wanted all those ridiculous plastic bags of things to be hidden away from my friends or for the floor to open up and swallow me for the time being. My mind was processing a lot at that time trying to make me a different person right there and then. I bet I did burn quite a few calories from all this intensity of emotion and thought. Another thought that was crossing my mind was that I could have used the money I had spent on many unnecessary items for something else. Not that it was a lot – to be fair, my budget was pretty humble anyway and I have been following my rule of not going into debt. Thank God. But still. I could have a bit of extra money that could be used in better ways.

D was there with me, and she took a picture of that disaster, but I made her delete it since, at that point, I did not want any recorded proof that would make me embarrass again in the future. Today, I wish we still had that picture. Damn it, I could have giggled again myself.

Now, when I am over it, I find it funny and even wish I could look at that picture and see all the progress I have made. Sometimes, a strong feeling of shame becomes a powerful trigger for improvement. If you can muster the courage to observe yourself honestly and critically, and if you combine it with a sense of humor, you will progress fast and efficiently.

With this in mind, I am glad that I had this experience in my life because it made me better, smarter, and stronger. I could have had all the best boxes to pack things properly and could have arranged to donate some things in advance. Still, then it's possible I would have missed this invaluable lesson triggered by my shameful realization: without all of those plastic bags, D's photos, and friends patiently carrying my stuff around and making jokes, I would have missed a tremendous opportunity to improve myself.

Since then, I have overall become a much more responsible buyer. Yes! That's the term: a responsible buyer is someone with a keen sense of buying the particulars on a need-only basis. It took me a big realization, an evening of embarrassment and shame, and then a good amount of analysis, self-reflection, and hard work to revisit my relationship with myself and consumption.

I started to look at consumption from different angles. I discovered a number of psychological triggers and insecurities that can lead to excess consumption and figured out the ways to hack into them and become a more balanced, confident, and happier person who has more time and money to do things they truly enjoy.

From the realization to the materialization of any idea, there is a long way to go, and I have been a work in progress all this time. When my journey in this direction started, I did not have a driver's license yet due to my unreasonable and ridiculous fear of the road test that I failed four or five times. I finally passed it recently - thank you, Heavens. I thought I would faint like one of those fainting goats, but somehow, the miracle happened.

So, before the Heavens eventually had mercy on me in this regard, I used to spend almost three hours a day on a subway when commuting to and from work. Armed with a notebook and a pen, I started writing down my thoughts that, over time, turned into a book draft. When I started working on my relationship with consumption, I also started noticing the consumption habits of others. I saw a lot of people in superstores and malls buying in bulk, putting the same thing twice or thrice in their cart, or leaving stores with big bags of similar-looking clothes. After a keen observation, I realized that perhaps I was not alone in being this type of work in progress and that perhaps some people would want to read my story and thoughts.

Maybe some people would find these useful or entertaining and just maybe they would like to share their stories and thoughts as well. So, after a few years of having the draft somewhere at the bottom of my drawer, I pulled it out and decided to grow a pair, if you may, and turn it into a book. Here we are!

# Introduction

Have you ever thought how we humans are the only mammal species that often communicate things we do not mean, do things we do not feel and buy things we do not need? Not that other mammals can buy things, but they tend not to pursue more food or items than they require for their living. While having evolved this far, we have also lost much of our substance and let shallowness overtake a big part of us.

Now, it is no secret that our relationship with things has much to do with our relationship with ourselves and others. To better understand this, all we need is a little introspection. We just have to look into ourselves, our hopes and dreams, insecurities and fears, stereotypes and illusions. I will share with you some that I had and ones I learned about. We will also take a brief look at the neuroscientific aspect of being such shallow beings.

In this book, I am focusing not on things you already have but on your desire to consume more—to purchase or acquire new things you will never need in life. The focus lies mainly on material things and belongings. But, I also mention things such as food and video games – with the focus, again, on the desire to obtain excessive amounts. My goal is to use a psychological, self-reflective, and logical approach, looking at the emotions that trigger behaviors and using fun examples – real and imaginary.

While I focus on clothing consumption as the main example here, no matter what kind of different items we may be consuming, the concept stays the same. It may be excessive consumption of new phones, watches, sports equipment, games, or even food – you name it. If you have at least once questioned your consumption habits and your relationship with things, this book should have something helpful for you.

As a reader, please note an important thing. Neither am I a professional in the subject of social sciences nor am I a neuroscientist. I am just a regular woman who found this topic important and did some analysis of it. I am sharing my own honest experience and thoughts, combined with some research and observations. My goal is to help you look at consumption and your relationship with things, yourself, and your life through the lens of various consumption triggers and see which ones resonate with you most. I believe this will inspire you to think more about the topic and find additional solutions that will work best for you. Thank you for choosing to read this book. I hope you enjoy it.

# Part I. Consumerism as an Attempt at a Quick Fix

## Chapter 1. There Are No Shortcuts for a Better Reality

### Hooked on Gratification

Another day started with a lack of sleep and an abundance of stress. I was tired and dissatisfied with the way things were going for me. I knew I wanted something else, something more than this. I had dark circles under my eyes, and my face was swollen – my mother had warned me before that a salty soup before bed was a bad idea as it makes your body accumulate water, but I was busy with school and work and a can of soup was all I had time for. And here I was, like a grumpy Hobbit taken out of his comfortable habitat and thrown into a busy and challenging reality.

The first three or four hours of the day, I spent fantasizing about being back in my warm bed. I felt miserable, only able to stay awake thanks to my favorite music, energetic and fast. It was also thanks to snacks – in every unclear or uncomfortable situation, I would reach for some chocolate, for which later at work, I earned my nickname as the Chocolate Princess or Chocolate Dealer, for offering it to others all the time.

I was so exhausted that I was shivering while everyone else was warm; I was swearing at myself for having stayed up late last night and swearing to myself that I would sleep for a long time as soon as classes and work were over. And then, of course, as it often happens, in the afternoon, I was as awake as I could be, and in the early evening, I was full of energy and curiosity and in the mood for all types of activities. The world is an interesting place, after all, especially when it is time to go to bed. And the same story repeated: I went to bed late, I woke up with difficulty, I swore to myself that it would not happen again, I cheered myself up with some more chocolate, pop, and music, and in the evening, I found a bunch of great things to do things that seemed way more interesting than sleep, and this cycle was continued until the week was over.

You can easily guess that by the end of the week, my body and mind were exhausted. With a busy schedule like that and not enough time to do basic chores during the week, I had to use my weekend to catch up on those household tasks and sleep. The constant rush left me feeling mentally drained, making it hard to enjoy any downtime. This was not giving me much time for high-quality emotional rewards, such as time with friends at an interesting event or activity or hobbies, which I have always had tons of. Instead, I had to clean the house, do laundry, grocery shop, cook, and do tons of accumulated assignments. And yes, sleep; though it was the most important above all, it was the least of my concerns.

Do you think our mind and nature care about these? Do you think they care about these artificial human-invented lifestyles, schedules, and needs? Does your nature stop requiring rewards, physical and emotional, just because you are too busy? No, it never does. The demands of life may distract us, but our bodies still crave balance and rest. The more we ignore these natural needs, the louder they become, often bursting as stress or fatigue that can't be easily handled. And when we do not have time for truly satisfying things to do and experience, we go for easy and instant rewards—ones that can be quickly and easily acquired.

And this is fair enough - your body has been waiting for these for a whole week and demands these now. Do you have time to arrange a hiking trip or a drawing session with your friends or to get the lifestyle you are dreaming of instantly? You do not. Then, you go for quick and short-term rewards that often come from the consumption of goods or addictive foods, excessive screen time, and other things. And from here, the problem begins. These instant pleasures can give temporary relief, but they often lead to feelings of emptiness. Also, relying on such pleasures often gives birth to the cycle of dissatisfaction where someone constantly feels dissatisfied and runs to achieve satisfaction in life. To an extent, you become an addict. Instead of solving the problem, you procrastinate, distracting yourself with these cheat codes for instant pleasure, leading to disappointment. You consume stuff, and it gives you positive emotions for a short period of time, instant gratification, and then you feel worse after, and you need more rewards to make yourself happy again.

Why would you feel bad after your instant gratification from consumption? Easy. You may have (again) spent more money than you should have, you may have given a word to yourself and did not keep it, you may have eaten food you know compromises your health or your desired weight, you may feel that you have wasted too much time on something, and so on. There may be a ton of other reasons. Basically, you feel guilt and failure. And crave more instant gratification to compensate for these hard feelings. And this puts you in a cursed circle of consumption. You keep chasing the illusion of lasting happiness, like thirsty travelers in the desert pursuing a distant mirage of water that's always just out of reach.

What we often end up doing is trying to use our will strength in an attempt to overpower our urge for gratification. What we do not fully understand is the power of this need that we naturally have for such gratification, stimulation, and dopamine. Did you know that a 1950s experiment demonstrated that rats would often press the lever to receive electrical stimulation to their brain rather than eat food? Our need for stimulation and gratification may, at times, be stronger than our survival needs and instincts, and this is when we approach the realm of addiction. We will briefly look into neuroscience later in the book. First, let's recognize our strong desire for stimulation and instant gratification. We can explore what drives our urge to consume and consider ways to manage it.

## Attempt at Substitution

There are so many examples we could possibly bring up as it relates to the topic of consumption as an attempt at substitution. For this little section, allow me to bring up one from a young city girl's life.

At eleven at night, Lisa came back home and threw her keys on the table. In fact, she had a designated place for the keys in her house, but the problem was that she was too tired and discouraged by the existing mess anyway. Priorities, right? Why waste time on putting things in their places when more fun things are waiting for you? Stuff was everywhere, and she did not know how to organize it — where on earth would she find space in her little apartment? Or perhaps she just did not bother to or was subconsciously afraid of facing the issue of overconsumption that she would need to admit to herself. She took off her red high-heeled shoes and put them among other shoes – some of which were also red with high heels but had a zipper or sparkles. Lisa was tired, and the next morning, she had to wake up early for work. Eleven at night was the earliest she could possibly make it back home without looking like a baby to her friends, who were or seemed to be the party animals and stayed up late. Why did she even go to that bar? Well, as she had so much stuff, she needed to show it off sometimes, right? So, that is why she went. And, of course, the girls took pictures. In fact, many pictures; they all kept taking pictures until everyone was satisfied with how they looked in one picture together – because all of them had something to show off on social media. Now, once it is uploaded, there is another race over there, the rat race of likes, comments, and online appreciation. So, in order to show off the stuff Lisa already had, she jumped into the cycle, which allowed her to be part of another cycle of instant gratification. So, while fulfilling one part of your instant gratification, you enter into another in an unnoticed manner.

You would think that Lisa is always like this – always paying too much attention to her looks and outfits. Well, she went on a vacation to a warm and beautiful place by the sea, among nature, with people she loved, doing things she loved to do. How much stuff do you think she took with her? Correct, a lot. A full luggage of stuff. Like many of us, she thought she would need all of those on her trip. A banana-coloured top? She would never survive without it, as it goes so well with her skin! Green pants? Of course! Two more pairs of similar pants? Sure, she can't discriminate. Dresses…. which should she take? Why not all of them? And let's not forget the accessories—she packed several pairs of shoes and a variety of jewelry to ensure she had the perfect look for every occasion! A common story for many of us. And then, surprisingly, while on vacation, she only used three or four outfits and hardly one of the few accessories she took. That's all. And she felt happy, truly happy and confident. She was in a place she loved, with people she cared about, doing things she enjoyed, and she felt at peace with herself. And she looked great! Who looks better than a happy healthy person, full of energy and charm?

I'm sure you realize that an addiction to consumption is a sign of something deeper that our mind and body are really craving and need. The vacation example has demonstrated to us that when we are happy and busy with what we love, material things become no more than mere instruments to us, and consumption loses much of its importance. At the same time, when you do not do things you love, getting stuff feels better because it is easier: we can buy it and obtain instant gratification. Changing your life requires way more effort and time. You have to wait for the result and have a lot of patience and strength of will to go through periods of hard work with few emotional rewards. And being stuck in a stressful routine makes this even more difficult. So, we seek instant and easy rewards, instant gratification, that can be obtained with money.

When you feel like compulsively consuming something, it may be a good idea to stop for a moment and ask yourself what it is that you would really like to be, to do, to feel, receive, or achieve, or what it is that you would like to hide from at the moment.

## It Is All About Your Reality.

Everything we do comes from our reality and is explained by it. I eat if I am hungry, I go to work because I need to make a living, and I go for a run every morning because I love it; it makes me healthier and fitter, and thus makes my reality better. I spend time with my friends because their company brings me joy and because we are there to help and support each other. I read books to learn new things and to escape to different worlds.

Now, why do we buy things? Yep, because we need them. We need a fridge, a microwave, furniture, bedding, and so many more things. But do we really need everything we buy? Have you ever bought something to never or hardly ever use it after? I don't know about you, but I must admit that I have, and definitely more than once. You look at an item and think, "Hell yeah, I need it! I will definitely need it!" And you come up with all those ideas of how you would use it, how it would look great in your home or garden, or on you, and how happy you will be. And then, guess what, you never even use it. And nothing changes in your life and in your reality. Just another item taking up space in your house. Just another reason to blame yourself for spending money, wasting time, and buying something you don't need. It makes you realize how easy it is to get caught up in the moment and forget what truly matters.

Everything we do is because we want to make our reality better in one way or another. It may not be conscious and may be dictated by our survival or primitive instincts, or it may be more elaborate than this. But it is to make our reality better or to serve our belief that this is good for us. This belief may be wrong; it may be a self-deceiving illusion, but even this illusion comes from your necessity to live a better reality. We often chase after things that promise happiness or fulfillment, thinking they will improve our lives. But, sometimes, it's the simplest things, like spending time with loved ones or enjoying nature, that truly bring us joy and contentment.

They say it is good to have a rich imagination. And so, it is indeed. Imagination helps create a better reality. However, it should not substitute reality or lead to a wrong perception of reality. Things go well when our imagination is on good terms with our sense of reality, and these two complement each other. It becomes hard and destructive when these two are in contradiction and when one chooses to see the world of their imagination instead of the world that it really is.

When we get ourselves a new piece of clothing to satisfy the urge we have, we tend to imagine our better selves in that piece. At least, this was what I was doing for a long time. If I had honestly pictured myself in that thing the way I was, with all the things I like and don't like about myself, perhaps I would not have bought it because it does not make any real difference. However, what I was imagining was a better me: me in better shape, with a better smile, with more confidence, and a better sense of style. This me was still to be made, not bought. I had to work out daily for a couple of months and cut out my favorite sweets and treats to get the shape I wanted; I actually had to get orthodontic treatment to get the smile I wanted. I went through a number of experiences and realizations in order to become a more confident person, and it took me some practice to improve my sense of style. And it was far from great in the past, believe me. Sometimes, I used to buy things that either made me look like an auntie, or a bit inappropriate for the situation, or were too big or small for me.

In university back home, sometimes my friends used to catch me on the stairs to save me from falling, as the heels I wore were not quite my size, as if learning to wear heels itself was not challenging enough. Yeah, I know. Bless their souls. Or, who knows, maybe I would have needed much more than orthodontic treatment should I have fallen from those stairs. Or there would have been nothing left to perform that orthodontic treatment on.

Anyway, I had to work on these things before there would be a difference. We cannot buy better selves, but we can become better selves through hard work and dedication. It takes time and effort to change our habits and mindset, but the results are worth it. By focusing on personal growth, we can find true satisfaction that lasts longer than any material possession. And as we make progress, we start to realize that fulfillment comes from within, not from what we own. Imagination does play a crucial role in this process. We need first to imagine a better self and then make steps towards it.

# Chapter 2. Trying to Buy an Illusion of a Better Self

Do you sometimes hate listening to a recording of your own voice? Or maybe seeing a video recording of yourself, or a picture taken randomly by a friend without you knowing it, where you did not make your classic charming face, and you look like you, but not you that you would like to see? I bet you did at least once have this feeling of disappointment and denial. Well, I have had these feelings for sure. And this is because we all imagine ourselves a certain way, and then we face reality.

The same applies to your life choices, actions, decisions, and feelings. You may have a certain view of an ideal self that you wish to be, and what you do may be going against it and threatening or ruining this self-perception. So, let's say you decided to live a healthy life and you are picturing yourself as a strong guy with a six-pack, but instead, you could not resist (again) having a few beers and fast food with your pals, and instead of that handsome guy with a six-pack you are now the proud owner of a beer belly, soft like a pillow. Nothing wrong with having this belly, but if you had imagined yourself as this guy with a six-pack that you were to soon become, with a healthy lifestyle to follow, an evening with beer not only made it more difficult for you to use your time and money for something else—and be the person you want to be—it also challenged your perception of yourself.

Let me give you another example, and this one is as familiar to myself as it is to many other people. You see a great piece of clothing, and maybe it is even on sale. And you go on imagining yourself in this beautiful outfit. You look great and feel great. Suddenly, even your life with this outfit seems better to you. You get it. You take it home. And then nothing changes in your life, absolutely nothing. More than that, you do not even look as great in this thing as you thought you would. You are the same you, with all your flaws, as before. And you experience disappointment. You are upset that you have spent more money and have bought more clothes when you already have more than enough and that you are not what you hoped you were. On top of that, you realize that the temporary thrill of the purchase fades quickly, leaving you feeling emptier than before. Each time you open your closet, it becomes a reminder of your unmet expectations.

When we buy something, we chase an illusion associated with the object we buy. When we buy something, we often try to get a new, upgraded identity. The fact that consumption gets triggered by illusions and a search for a better self and that these illusions often lead to disappointment is a powerful thing. I was talking about this from the beginning –consumption of another unnecessary purchase leaving you guilty and upset.

## There are no shortcuts for a better self.

To be completely honest, when I was buying numerous shirts, skirts, and shoes, I was imagining a better me wearing these and looking great. This better me was more fit, had better posture, better make-up skills, and a sense of style, and was a happier and better individual in general. This was a little different person who I still needed to become through much work and improvement. But we subconsciously look for shortcuts and hacks to make our lives easier. So, instead of working on reality, we often try to imagine or even buy illusions. And when we see that this beautiful cover, this magical instrument of change that we were secretly hoping would make our life better, did not change the content, and when we see the same monkey in a different costume, we get disappointed. This adds to the sense of guilt we get from spending money, wasting time, and so on, and results in the fact that we feel even worse than before purchasing the thing, and we need our next reward to make us feel better and to make us 'better.' And eventually, we find ourselves trapped in the cycle of craving and disillusionment.

## There are no shortcuts when it comes to your hobbies and skills.

Similarly, we want to be better at what we do. We want to work better, write better, dance better, play music better, and so on. We want a reality where we do all these things better. Confession time for me: As I started learning belly dancing, I remember buying a few colorful belly dance belts and tops. It felt like I was becoming a better dancer just by surrounding myself with these things and creating a belly dance environment in my small room by hanging these beautiful belts on the sides of my bookshelves and staring at them while doing other things. Now, while these did motivate me to practice more, they still did not improve my skills simply with their presence in my wardrobe. For that, I needed to practice, practice, and practice more. I remember having a couple of belly dance student performances in restaurants where we did dance compositions in groups. I asked my brother and sometimes my friends to record me. When I watched these later, I had to admit that the main thing that made it look like I was belly dancing was my shiny and colorful outfit with little ringing bells, while my body was putting way less effort into those moves than it was supposed to. Since then, when I practise belly dance moves, I dress as simply as possible, to not get distracted by costumes. I am still a beginner, and I am facing it. Now, I know that true growth comes from within, not from the glitter around me.

I know it is also common that people learning to play guitar often go for fancier guitar equipment and pedals instead of upgrading their skills first through a lot of daily practice. They look for things that will make it possible for them to bring diversity into their play, while the number one thing that will give them all the diversity they want is their skill. Once you have good skills, you can get all the things needed and be a rockstar. Of course, it is up to them if they prefer to get these earlier on as they practice—as long as these things do not substitute the amount of practice and do not shift their focus. The excitement of new gear can lead to a temporary boost in motivation, but it often fades when real progress requires consistent effort. Developing a strong foundation through consistent effort will not only improve their playing but also help them appreciate the gear they choose to invest in later.

Now, how about golf? I have always been fascinated by all the calm patience that golf players possess. I am pretty bad at golf. I would get impatient quickly, hit this stubborn ball like I am mad at it, and then go look for it all over the bushes and ditches later. To be fair, I have only played it about three times in my life so far. Anyhow, someone who is much better at golf than I am said that it is also a common theme for some golf players to buy expensive golf equipment with more dedication than they work on actually improving their skills.

So, let's not look for shortcuts with anything. They only confuse you and take you further from your goals. Instead, accept the journey and commit to consistent practice. Just remember that true growth comes from efforts and patience, not from quick fixes.

## Be Honest with Yourself.

*"Now one-half of his abilities is devoted to deceiving himself, and the other to justifying the deceit."*

*– Anna Karenina, by Leo Tolstoy.*

If your friend came to you in a fancy car, wearing stunningly fashionable clothes, but then sat next to you, hunched over the table, with sad and tired eyes, telling you their life was going great, would you believe them? What if an old friend came to you shining and smiling, full of energy, in the same old shirt of five years? Which one of these two people is living the life they want? And which of the two looks better and makes a better impression? You tell me.

Not all things are equally important. Some things have a much bigger impact than others. Health, mood, and what is going on in your life are much more significant than what is hanging on your body or carrying your body from place to place, and, believe it or not, much more noticeable, too. Prioritizing your well-being leads to a more fulfilling life. When you feel good inside, it naturally shines through in everything you do.

If you can have it all, good for you, enjoy. However, we often face situations where we need to choose and prioritize. And this has everything to do with not only our time and money but also with our energy and attention. Nobody can tell you what you should be putting your attention, time, energy, and money into. And this is the point. You decide what and where you want to place your focus in this life. Not anyone else, not society or its expectations, not social stereotypes of status and prestige. Just you! And this is liberating. Once you realize this, you will naturally go the way your heart and mind want to. And for this, you need to know very well your real self, the one that may be hiding under multiple layers of superficial things, manners, stereotypes, insecurities, and fantasies. When you deeply understand yourself, it empowers you to make choices that are aligned with your values and goals; otherwise, you will end up making decisions based on society and its fake expectations, as well as your inner insecurities and search for a quick fix.

A key part is to be brutally honest with yourself. Listen, you are to enjoy your own company twenty-four hours a day, seven days a week, and there is no escape. Do you really think you should be trying to impress yourself with pretty tales about yourself? As if you were going to leave yourself or not talk to yourself for a while if you were not impressed. Come on. Good luck with that! Be completely honest with yourself. Take pride in your achievements, acknowledge your flaws, and work on improving them. Always strive to make your life better overall. And when you find a problem, work on its solution, not on its decoration. Go all-in. You are always by your side, so you better be your own best friend.

Sometimes, or even often, we do not want to face the truth, consciously or subconsciously. We want to think that we are a better person or at a better spot in life than we actually are. But how can we reach our goals if we don't clearly understand where we are right now? Remember those Math tasks at school where someone heads from point A to point B? How would you identify the route and find a solution if you do not know where point A is? Now, let's say Peter does not like his point A. He wishes it was 50 miles south of where it is. Now, good luck making it to point B using the route you would take if you were at a different place originally.

When you honestly recognize where you are, even if you don't like it, avoid getting upset with yourself. Imagine if Peter, when heading from point A to point B, did not like where point A was and expressed his frustration for half an hour before heading to point B. He then stopped every now and then on his way to express some more frustration. How long would it take Peter to get to point B? Definitely longer than if he just walked calmly, right? Same with you and me – things take longer when, instead of just working on them, we go all dramatic.

Another danger of deceiving yourself is that it would lead to you building a whole alternative reality in your head around the original lie to protect it from any attack by reality. This would create even more distortion and confuse you more. So, instead of moving your point A in your mind 50 miles south from where it actually is, you would move it 300 miles southeast and have inaccurate maps of roads in the whole area. Good luck making it to your point B. Not only would you not make it to point B easily, if ever, but you would not be seen by others to be where you perceive yourself to be, which would lead to more confusion and stress and, among other things, more cravings for instant gratification and impulsive behaviors.

## The Devil is in the Details

Now that we have identified points A and B, it matters to know what is in between. In my university years, I remember having an oil painting session with a friend in my dormitory room. We were watching a video tutorial and trying to follow as the painter was creating beautiful scenery. The thing about many of such tutorials is that, while being very helpful, they also often skip on whole parts of the process. You go through a step-by-step, and then suddenly, the screen shows something that definitely requires more steps in between. Missing these key steps can leave us confused and unsure, just like skipping vital parts of any journey from point A to point B. Like, you were drawing lines in pencil to mark where the river and the trees are, and then boom - you hear that now that all the curvy details are in, we are moving to the next step. What curvy details? When were we doing them? You rewind the video back a bit to see if you missed anything, but no, the video didn't show you how to make these lines into actual tree outlines. The previous video frame with clear lines dissolved right into a frame with hills and trees in it. You don't know whether to feel disappointed with the video as it skipped an important part of the process or with yourself as maybe it was supposed to be an easy part, and you were supposed to figure it out yourself. So, feeling a little let down with a touch of stupid, we proceeded to draw those curvy details on our own. The result was different from what we saw on the screen, and the difference was not in our favor. The more we continued with the video and its instructional gaps, the more our paintings deviated from the result we aimed for. Somewhere around the midpoint, we laughed at our masterpieces that could easily pass as ten-year-olds work and decided to do something else instead.

It is important to be consistent and not skip any steps or stages of the process you're going through. For this, it is crucial to have a clear direction in mind with specific plans. You cannot just say to yourself that you would work towards a healthier diet without adding specifics, such as what it is that you would be eating, what it is that you would avoid, and how much and when you would be eating these. You cannot decide to declutter your space without putting specific timelines on it and planning the details. This includes which parts of the house you would be declutter first, when and how you would be doing it, etc. Neither can you succeed in limiting your spending on certain types of items without setting clear numerical values and timelines. And so on. This principle applies to everything. The devil is in the details.

## Address the Right Problem.

When I was a teenager, among areas of improvement for me were my posture and sense of style. Where would you have recommended I start from? Probably posture, right? Because it is much more significant and has a bigger impact on health and looks. And also, because it takes more time and consistent effort to bring it in order. Plus, good posture can boost confidence and influence how others perceive you. Improving posture can also prevent potential health issues later in life. Well, if we think more about it, we can say that posture itself may be a result of self-confidence, which in turn may be increased through making yourself look good by dressing up. Legit. It may mean that doing both at the same time would also be a good idea. What we can agree on, however, is that most of the focus, effort, and attention should be directed toward improving posture and the various factors that influence it, right?

I have known guys who were young, good-hearted, and hard-working. What they could work on were their social skills. These people didn't get enough attention from their peers or the people they were interested in, making them feel shy and awkward around them. I genuinely believed that the best thing for them to do, if possible, would be to get in great shape, feel healthier and more confident, and go hang out with more people on a daily basis, do more things with people to improve their social skills. However, I have seen guys work day and night in order to afford expensive cars, just to make a better impression on others. In my opinion, this was not the best choice they could have made. Working a lot to get ahead in life would sound like a great thing to do. However, working all the time just for these cars as an instrument to impress others, may not be a wise exchange of time and energy for an outcome. It meant even less time socializing with people, so they were depriving themselves of an opportunity to improve their social skills. It also means less time exercising, not getting enough sleep, and, likely, not having a very healthy diet because it also requires time and resources. Getting a fancy car may be a good thing on its own if you love it, but if this is how you are planning to get attention and human interaction, you should not forget that the people you want around you are those who would first like your personality and not your car unless you would like to become a gold-digger magnet.

So, in short, for you to be better with people, you should be with people and should be there for them – and there is no other shortcut for sincere human interaction. A car is great, but it won't get you a true friend out of nowhere. This is not how it works. If you would like great posture and shape, you should be working on exercise, diet, and whatever works. But not fancy clothes on top of something you yourself do not want to see in the mirror. Improving yourself for real is not covering up the same body and mind with new things. Developing healthy habits takes time and commitment, which leads to lasting changes. It's important to build confidence from within rather than relying on external resources.

# Chapter 3. Consumption for Consolation or Escape

## Emotional or Physical Discomfort

There is this time interval in spring when I tend to consume junk food and unnecessary goodies more than during any other time period throughout the year. Not that it is a legit excuse, but the reason is me seeking to compensate for the discomfort I feel and my inability to distract myself with healthier and more meaningful things and activities. Thank you, seasonal allergies. You were not welcome here but yet you came to stay. During those months, I sneeze constantly, so much so that I'm sure I burn calories just from sneezing. My nose itches and feels bigger than it actually is, and my eyes are watery, making it look like I'm always crying about everything.

Sometimes, all this messes with my voice, and I think I could do a voice-over for a cartoon character. I can now admire cherry blossoms only by looking at the images online, and even that sometimes makes me give out a sneeze or two and rub my nose. The poor thing goes through a lot during spring times; I am grateful it is still there. And there is little relief from allergy medications. I feel feverish and dizzy, have a headache, and overall feel like I have had the bad flu non-stop for quite a few weeks. Since I can't engage in any interesting activities or do many meaningful things beyond what's necessary. I often indulge in addictive, sugary, or savory foods. I also drink soda, play video games or games on my phone from time to time, and buy unnecessary items that make me feel good. These distractions help fill the gap when I'm not able to do anything more fulfilling.

All of us feel unwell from time to time, and some people unfortunately tend to have serious problems with their health. When you are unwell, it is very difficult to go for action-based gratification or invest much time and effort into something. Besides, the very fact of being unwell can make you crave consolation and easier emotional rewards. How many times did you crave something material or yummy after a painful visit to a dentist? I remember buying a number of things I did not particularly need after such visits throughout my life. This behavior often stems from a desire to escape discomfort and seek temporary happiness. In the end, while these small treats might offer relief, they don't address the underlying issues causing the discomfort.

Not only physical discomfort and pain have this effect, but emotional uneasiness does, too. Don't we tend to console ourselves with stuff or treats – be those some sweets or beers, - when we are low, stressed, have a bad day, or are frustrated or lost? The mechanism behind these is the same – we search for instant gratification, as discussed in the previous chapter. And the right tip here would be to keep this in mind and be careful at times like that. You may want to acknowledge to yourself that this time period of pain or stress will somewhat suck for you anyway, and you do not need to desperately shower yourself with instant gratification gifts and behaviors as you may regret this later. Remember, this hard time shall pass, and the sun will shine. So, maybe if you do use these, do so in moderation. I will talk about such challenging times later in the book when I bring goats into the picture.

## Lack of Safety, Stability, or Control

In a life where we do not know what comes tomorrow and little seems stable or safe, we tend to bring in something that does seem safe and stable. We tend to look for shortcuts subconsciously; this often happens through stuff. When your home is filled with things you know will not run away from you and that nobody will be taking from you, you may feel safer inside, often without even realizing it. When you know that the next day, and the week after, and three months from now, all these items will be where you want them to be, you feel more stable. Surrounding yourself with more stuff may give you a false sense of safety and stability. Having a home with your stuff may feel like marking your territory and your presence. Besides, it feels like no matter what happens next, you do have some possessions and belongings that you can use. However, this accumulation of items can also lead to clutter, which may create stress and overwhelm instead of comfort. Ultimately, true security comes from within, not from the things we own.

Accumulating possessions and clutter (that would follow if you consume too much) are also believed by psychologists to be a way for people to deal with their trauma, as these are something constant that is always there, carries memories, and often even subconsciously constitutes a part of a person's identity. If you think this may be relevant to you, there are plenty of resources on the internet, including YouTube, that can help you start exploring the topic.

You know how animals build their little homes underground where they store supplies for the winter? What if we have a similar instinct? We may accumulate things to feel safe. We seem to forget that even if all clothes stores were to close down tomorrow, with what you already have in your wardrobe, you will be OK and not end up naked. You will make it until the stores open up again, believe me. And, wait, stores are not closed! They are available on every corner of your town. Hey, then you have absolutely nothing to worry about and no need to rush and buy things. Just saying. Taking a moment to appreciate what you already own can lead to greater contentment.

It is our anxiety that pushes us towards accumulating and keeping items that we may potentially use one day. I remember how oftentimes, when I would see an item in a store, I would think of possible situations when I would possibly need it – even if such situations were far ahead or never coming my way. These wide, dark, waterproof pants with big pockets? Oh yes! I will need them for all kinds of hiking, camping, sports, and casual outdoor events. That very elegant dress? It would go super well at a fancy party. Those pink earrings? If I ever wear a certain type of dress – that I do not have yet – these will look great with it. And I wanted those right then as if all the stores would be closed the day after. The whole city's stores and malls were to vanish, and I would be left with what I had accumulated by then. And as if in such a scenario, these things would even matter. Or as if I would be given such short notice for an event that I would only get enough time to reach for the item in my wardrobe and put it on. I believe that somewhere deep inside, I was preparing myself to be ready for anything at any time, which is a sign of some inner anxiety and seeking the feeling of safety.

The paradox is that consuming things out of anxiety leads to more anxiety. The more you buy and accumulate, the more you have to earn to pay for these belongings, the more you have to work in order to earn more — the less freedom of time and money you have. If you lack time, energy, and financial resources, how can you be safer and more secure? Let's say you have few belongings – only what you really need and love – and have more money, energy, and time. Then, you can technically change your life at any point you would like — to move, change your job, travel, take a break, learn a new skill, etc. Time and energy (health) are our main resources that determine whether we can feel safe and secure and move towards our goals. Combined with financial independence, these are what we should aim for, as they can bring us where we want to be. Having fewer possessions can lead to a simpler, less stressful life, allowing you to focus on what truly matters, such as relationships and personal growth.

What lies between this realization and our desperate necessity for security and stability? I believe that it is admitting that absolute security and stability do not exist, ever. Life is such an unpredictable and complicated combination of multiple factors that there is literally no way you can ever be sure your life is going to be safe and stable today, tomorrow, or at any point in time. Once you admit this, you may feel uneasy at first, but then this realization will be liberating. It allows us to embrace change and focus on personal growth rather than being paralyzed by the fear of what might happen. And, instead of hiding behind something that supposedly makes you feel more secure, you will go towards learning to stand on your feet again every time you fall, explore, achieve, and improve.

Consuming also gives you a feeling of being in control. Buying something is within your control, as well as taking care of your belongings. Because many of us fear losing control over our lives, we may unconsciously look for ways to prove to ourselves that we are in control. While having some control is great, it is important to understand that life is all about things that happen out of nowhere, coincidences, and a lot of factors that make our full control of life impossible. And, to be fair, isn't this what makes life much more captivating? In my opinion, it is the real crux of life.

We should let go of things we do not have any control over. When I worked at a call center, we once had a customer who forgot his password and hated all the temporary passwords he was sent. When he learned that these were generated automatically by the system and could be changed to anything he wanted, he began to hate the agents, too. It seemed like the gentleman wanted so much to be in control that he failed to get the actual problem solved. He ended up changing agents, stressing and screaming, and sending us all one by one to hell. The man did not realize that even if all of us had followed his directions and gone to hell and back, bringing him magnets from there, the temporary password would still be automatically generated by the system. Refusing to let go of something he could not control, the man chose to give up his access to the system and lose his money. And I bet that he himself, as well as all of us, were extremely exhausted at the end of this lovely communication.

There are a lot of things we cannot control. But therein lies the beauty of life—its unpredictability allows us to let go and enjoy experiencing life's turns. And, of course, we should take better control of areas and things that we can. Accepting this unpredictability easily leads you to personal growth as you learn to adapt to new situations. Focusing on what we can control helps reduce anxiety and stress, allowing us to appreciate the present moment more fully.

## When Your Head is not in the Right Place, from Stress

The clock was ticking, and the assignment deadline was just around the corner. If only my 3D modeling and animation software were cooperating. Instead, though, it was a mess, and my character's head and arms were suddenly shown as growing right out of his bottom. That was not an artistic trick. I never meant for the character to miss out on his torso, neck, and other useful goodness and have his head and arms come directly out of his soft part. How would you even make a good salsa dance animation with this?

One of the stressful things about studying digital skills, like, for example video game design and animation, is that sometimes things that are supposed to work just don't. This can be frustrating, especially when you've invested a lot of time and effort into a project. As a newbie in the field, you try to figure out whether you messed up somewhere or it is the software that is, for some reason, hallucinating, and a simple restart could help. Sometimes, it feels like a game of trial and error, leaving you wondering if you're cut out for this or not. On other occasions, the whole thing freezes and if you were not saving your progress every several minutes, you may have to redo what you thought you had successfully completed. In my case, it was all three things at the same time - weird anatomy, a frozen screen, and regret for not saving my progress properly before the character's upper body somehow collapsed into his bottom, and the screen froze, unable to handle the traumatizing look of the whole thing.

After releasing a roar of an injured beast, I decided to give my computer a few more minutes in the hope that it would unfreeze and get the character's head out of his bottom, literally. To cope with the stress and helplessness, I went for instant gratification. Out of nowhere, in the blink of an eye, a couple of chocolate bars with some soda ended up on my desk, and on my phone, a bunch of colorful balls started appearing on the screen as I was arranging them in rows by color. At that moment, the sweetness of chocolate and the fun of the game provided a quick escape. What is worse, I also remembered that I needed to order a specific item online. I did order it. And not only it. As a subconscious compensation for the stress, combined with impatience and desire to hide from reality, I also impulsively bought some other things that I did not really need.

For those concerned about the character's anatomy, it ended up being just fine after I eventually turned the computer off and back on, restarted the software, and redid completely about fifty steps or so. But the damage was done. It seemed as if this whole head-in-the-ass thing was contagious, and for some time, I could not locate my head where it was supposed to be, figuratively speaking.

In situations where, in addition to stress, we also feel helplessness and lack of control, especially when these are made worse by the need to hurry and deliver a result, we may find ourselves hiding from reality through one or another type of consumption. This can lead to impulsive buying or unhealthy habits, which only provide temporary relief. Instead of facing the situation, we distract ourselves, creating a cycle that makes us feel even worse in the long run. But, if we realize this, we can make better choices, solve problems more efficiently, and manage our stress differently. It's important to recognize these patterns and find healthier ways to cope, like talking to someone or taking a break to clear our minds. By doing so, we can regain control and work towards our goals more effectively.

## Procrastination and Perfectionism

*"Procrastination is like a credit card: it's a lot of fun until you get the bill,"*

*– Christopher Parker, actor.*

Just like we borrow money from our future selves by using credit cards, we take time from our tomorrow selves by procrastinating. And money, too. Procrastination often leads to compulsive consumption. The stress caused by procrastination leads to restless discomfort, which, in turn, makes you crave instant gratification. The biggest amounts of snacks I consumed and unnecessary items I treated myself to usually happened when I was stressed or unhappy about something, and often when there was something I needed to do, something that seemed big and intimidating, and that I was procrastinating on. During these times, I'd find myself playing some games online or mindlessly scrolling through shopping websites, convincing myself I deserved a little treat to feel better. I can remember binge-watching shows with a pile of snacks beside me, all while avoiding the work that was looming over my head.

While I was writing my master's thesis, I remember a lot of impulsive snacking. This was due to the lack of sleep and stress coming from procrastination. Thesis writing was a process that I could not see an end to. Especially as my curiosity was pushing me to dig into more and more resources on my topic, I was drowning in all that good stuff that I found in four to five different languages and that I had no idea where the heck I was to put in my thesis. Even my supervisor was telling me to stop digging and focus on the material I already had.

Was it perfectionism? Yes, perhaps. In fact, I believe that perfectionism and procrastination are related. When you aim for a good enough result, you can get it done quicker and with less stress. Letting go of the need for perfection can relieve unnecessary pressure. If you act from a perfectionism standpoint, the scale of the thing you expect yourself to accomplish scares the hell out of you, and your whole being tries to hide from it. This fear often leads to avoidance and procrastination, making it even harder to start. Instead of focusing on progress, you get stuck worrying about meeting unrealistically high standards set by your own-self for yourself. Furthermore, you do not even know what the scale of the thing actually is since there is no limit to perfection. You literally do not know where to stop and often do so only when the deadline comes, and you simply have no more time to add to your project. Heck, even while writing this book, I can't bring myself to finish the draft, as my inner perfectionist won't stop looking for more I can do and improve on it. I am exhaling, facepalming, but writing on.

While one part of your brain is this perfectionist, the rest of the brain and body are in a state of stress. "What the heck," they think to themselves in their way. Something does not feel right, and we snap into impulsive behaviors. This disconnect can lead to unhealthy coping mechanisms, such as overeating or spending money on things we don't need. Instead of addressing the underlying stress, we seek quick distractions that only provide temporary relief.

It is not only buying things or eating like no tomorrow. It can be gaming for hours while you know that you have to get something done, but instead, keep your presence in the virtual world of kingdoms, quests, or battles. This escape can feel more appealing than dealing with the stress of real-life responsibilities. I have been there, too, building Egyptian and Greek cities and clicking on their inhabitants to hear whether they were happy instead of building on my projects and making sure I was happy about where I was in life. This distraction took away precious time I could have used to work towards my own goals and find fulfillment in my life. Instead, I found myself stuck in a loop of virtual achievements while my real-life aspirations went unaddressed.

So, what do we do with perfectionism and procrastination? First of all, we do not procrastinate on finding solutions, and second, we do not go into perfectionism while solving them. Just kidding. Instead of looking for perfect solutions and delaying any change, we should just get started and make adjustments as we go along. I find it helpful to break projects into smaller, specific steps and celebrate each of these accomplishments. To many people, it feels good to check boxes on their to-do lists. This takes the uncertainty and scale out of the equation and makes things much more precise and more combined of little steps, each very accomplishable. Before you know it, you will have most of your project done.

Another thing that helps me is keeping in mind my following projects – ones that I will be starting after this one is complete.

This also removes the endless timeline for me because the sooner I finish one task, the sooner I can move on to the next. It could be something enjoyable or something I really need to tackle.

Whether it's a necessity or the desire for gratification, either way, motivates me to get my current task done quickly. There's no room for perfectionism or procrastination. Good-enough and soon-enough are what I go for. I can improve on my results later. It is better than never getting anything done.

Please also note that both extreme perfectionism and procrastination may often be caused by trauma, including childhood trauma. Understanding this link can help people be kinder to themselves. By recognizing the reasons behind these behaviors, individuals can work on them more effectively and begin to heal. If you think this may relate to you, please consider exploring the topic and reaching out to specialists if needed. These may have to do with feeling not enough and with a freeze response.

## Lack of Sense of Meaning

I remember reading a short motivational line somewhere that stated something like this: Focus on your personality, not possessions, for when you die, people will remember you for what you did, not what you had. They may say, "So sad! He or she was a great person!" Nobody will say: "Such a tragedy! What an expensive couch he or she had!"

Indeed, the meaning does not lie in our possessions as much as it does in our actions and personalities. People will look at you in a certain way depending on what you are as a human being and what characteristics you possess in interaction with them. This connection is often built on mutual respect, kindness, and authenticity. Ultimately, lasting relationships and a positive reputation are formed through genuine interactions rather than material things. And, as we have already discussed, it does not matter too much to you either. Do what you should do and what you love; spend time with your loved ones and take care of people around you. However, we often hide behind our stuff and look for meaning in our possessions.

I remember when I was in grade two or three, colorful plastic playcaps and yo-yo toys were very popular among my classmates and my generation in general. Children were collecting different caps and badges with cartoon or movie characters and comparing and exchanging these with each other every day. At some point, having more caps could make you a more popular kid than having good character – for a short while. Through collecting all these items, you also felt more meaningful to your peers, and yourself. This focus on possessions, however, often overshadowed the importance of kindness and friendship. Eventually, many realized that authentic connections come from shared experiences and genuine relationships rather than material items. This was a regular part of a typical child's play, and there was nothing wrong with it. But it shows how possessions can sometimes play a role in our sense of meaning.

This next story was told to me by a friend about one of his friends; I have modified it a bit. A grown-up guy was collecting all types of superhero dolls he could find and was placing them in some unique ways that had meaning to him and then reorganizing them again and again as new ones appeared. He looked forward to every new day and week to search for and collect more of these. If the guy was happy with this, I would just say that this is his hobby, and there is absolutely nothing strange about it – we all have our hobbies and preferences. However, the reality was that he constantly felt sad and lonely – except for those times when he would get his next doll and place it on the right shelf. He would want to show this off to someone, and interestingly, his desire to talk to people would grow when he had such accomplishments to share and a topic to discuss. It may be my friend's and my wild guess, but we both thought this guy felt like he needed validation and was trying to get it through his collection. It was as if he was finding meaning for himself through these items and felt the need to keep adding more to them. This guy was a good man and was loved by his friends for what he was and would have been loved by more people should he have let them into his life. However, he kept seeking meaning through stuff – not positive actions and interactions.

Perhaps what happens with a sense of meaning is somewhat similar to rewards – you can get these through positive action, work, communication, and relationships, or you can get yourself in a circle of material consumption. When people focus on meaningful experiences, they often feel more fulfilled and connected to others, which leads to greater happiness. In contrast, relying on material possessions for meaning can lead to a temporary high that quickly fades, leaving a sense of emptiness and dissatisfaction.

## Self-Sabotage Through Consumption

Did it ever occur to you that by buying excessive things, you are not as rewarding as you are punishing and self-sabotaging yourself? This wild thought woke me up once and kept me awake for a few minutes. It didn't let me fall back asleep until I left a note on my smartphone for myself to come back to later. Think about it this way – when we buy things, we spend money; when we spend money, we do not save money; when we do not save money, we do not allow ourselves to get something more significant – be it a house or another asset, traveling experience, or profit from wise investments. As I was lying in the dark with my eyes wide open as if I was watching out for a monster who lives under the bed to come out, I realized that we often act like we do not deserve to save money for something bigger, something we truly want, like we cannot reach our bigger goals. According to statistics, most branded items are consumed by people of lower and middle class. It almost feels like while we may be faking the lifestyle we want, deep inside, we do not believe we deserve it or belong there. We, therefore, spend all we have before, God forbid, we actually make it happen. This behavior reflects a fear of success and an internal struggle with self-worth. Almost as if this would undermine our identity and internal stability. Wild thought, isn't it? Wild but largely accurate, as I see it.

And elaborating more on this and looking deep inside, I understood that this also relates to new items we do not use. We often buy things that we consider great, but deep inside, we feel we do not deserve them, or, at least, 'not today'; we then do not use these items and buy new ones similar to the ones we already have. We buy good items but do not allow ourselves to use them, subconsciously deeming ourselves not worthy of them or feeling too shy to use them. Then, at some point, we want to bring this little upgrade into our life and, forgetting that we already have this kind of item, we buy another one, only to not allow ourselves to use it. So, you may spend your time and money on similar items a few times without letting yourself use them. Thus, you sabotaged yourself twice – one, by not deeming yourself deserving of such an upgrade, and two – by spending all this money that you could have saved towards something you truly want (and probably subconsciously consider yourself unworthy of as well).

So, what do we do? Well, I made a rule for myself where I use items as soon as possible upon buying them. If I do not feel comfortable doing so and cannot clearly define a real event or situation when the items will be used, I will be donating or selling them. This way, I can declutter my space while also ensuring that items go to someone who will appreciate and make use of them. I say to myself, 'If I do not deserve it, someone else does.' Wouldn't this phrase make you 'ouch' inside? This is the point. Once the item is set aside for donation or sale, you might change your perspective on the item and yourself and start using it. Or, if not, give it away and never look back. To be fair, some items are just not your style or do not fit your lifestyle, anyway. They will definitely fit someone else's.

# Part II. Building Consumerism Resistance

---

## Chapter 1. Free Yourself from Unnecessary Judgement

### Who Cares? | This is NOT Important

When I was little, we used to travel every summer. On the airplanes, there were these little two-dimensional paper entertainment pieces for little passengers, where boys could assemble a little aircraft while girls were offered a doll to dress in different outfits. You were just taking a paper dress and attaching it to a paper doll, then you would take pants and a shirt, and you go on and on until you got bored. Then, you might ask your brother to trade toys and play with an airplane. However, he wouldn't be very interested in dressing up a doll because, as he said, it didn't involve building anything or making interesting changes; it was just the same thing. And he was right: it was the same face with a different outfit, the same shape, in a different color. There was a difference, but it was so small compared to the one you would get when you exchange dolls with another girl passenger and dress her in your paper dresses. The real difference was the one between dolls, not between outfits. And you would wait for your brother to finish playing with the aircraft so that you can also do that and actually make a change and build something.

It works in a very similar way with humans. The way we look, as well as feel and act, makes much more of a difference than what outfits we wear. I am not saying that outfits are not important at all – they are to a certain extent – but we definitely overestimate their importance and underestimate the importance of our personality, mood, fitness level, confidence, and other things that cannot be bought but made through hard work. We need to understand that we should first improve the doll and then go for new outfits, or we should even build first - if many core changes are required in our lives. Then we go through some construction work first before we can go on to the decoration stage. Only then can we truly appreciate and enjoy the results of our efforts.

While you may be thinking about what other shirt to buy or what hairstyle to try, let me tell you a little secret. A person or people you are trying to be attractive or interesting to do not care about these things as much as you think they do. Really. Proven by a large number of my male and female friends, I have made my guinea pigs and asked a bunch of questions on the topic. In fact, some of these guys were even surprised why there *would* be such questions in the first place. How does it matter how much stuff you have? Or if your hair is straight or curled today. Why would anyone care too much about your necktie? You have worn the same dress for the last several parties. Oh really? That is the end of the world. How can you even show your face to people now, you barbarian! Seriously, guys, even my brother did not realize I wear earrings at all until several years after I got my ears pierced, and I asked him for advice on which ones to wear. I think this says it all, no? He *has always noticed* whenever I was happy or upset, healthy or unwell, in or out of good shape, behaving well or messing things up, interesting or boring to be around, etc. He would also notice if I looked generally good or not. In fact, it is when we do not look good is when people start looking into the details of why what is wrong, whereas if we look good, they often won't even remember the next day what we were wearing. Unless sometimes when we look exceptionally good in a certain outfit.

Think of your first date with your significant other. Or the date when you fell for each other. I bet you now do remember what they were wearing, and they remember your outfit. But this is not because of the outfit but rather because of you and their feelings for you. This is what makes your outfit on that day special to them. My significant other was wearing a T-shirt and shorts, and I was wearing a shirt, jeans, and a denim jacket. Nothing fancy, but we remember how we stared at each other and thought about how great the other one looked.

Unlike dolls or mannequins, we have a character and so much more about us than just a look. And our look itself is much more than outfits. Let's do some Math here: if your nature and character constitute 50% (let's just say that) and the whole appearance aspect the other 50%, then a piece of outfit can be somewhere between 1% and 30% of your appearance. It cannot go higher than that unless it looks so terrible on you that it changes you completely. So, let's take the maximum of 30% out of the maximum of 50% - we are getting a little over 15%. So, at most 15% of your perception by others may depend on your outfit detail. Again, unless you mess it up so bad that the only thing they see is that ridiculous out-of-place thing, like a mini-mini skirt at a job interview or a bright neon necktie with pink shoes. So, as reasonable human beings, should we focus on 15% or 85%? Of course, these were rough calculations that you can argue with, but this was to give you a general idea, a proportion, and a right scale.

People generally do *not* over-analyze the behaviors of others. And most of the time they see what they are shown. So, if you try to picture yourself from the outside, you won't see in that image all the internal worries, doubts, or insecurities. This means that others may be more focused on their perceptions than on judging you. How many times have you worn unmatched socks? I have done it quite often – when I do not get my laundry done on time, and I have to combine those single socks whose couples sadly and mysteriously disappeared. They are now single and ready to mingle. It would probably be a rather silly thing to do if I knew I would be taking my shoes off somewhere. However, if I wear shoes and nobody can see my different socks, why would I care? It is not like I am hurting anyone by wearing unmatched socks. So, my message here is not to encourage you to wear unpaired socks - I think you do it anyway, from time to time, even if you don't admit it – but to show you that many things we worry about because we think that other people notice them, actually cannot be seen. Or they do not matter. For example, do you look carefully at your friend trying to find that tiny stain on the right sleeve of their sweater? Do you spend minutes trying to figure out whether their car, iPhone, bag, or dress is very new? If you don't, then guess what? They don't either. Or if they do and this affects their opinion of you, do you want someone like this in your life? Remember, what truly matters is how you feel about yourself and what you are as a person, not what others think. Focus on your connections and experiences rather than on superficial judgments.

There are a number of tasks and actions that we perform on a daily basis. And to a big extent we are perceived by others depending on things we do. If you are happy with the things you do, then you should not worry. Your type of people will also be happy about it – and why bother trying to please people who are not your type? If there is something you yourself would like to change and improve, go for it. Focus on aligning your actions with your values, and you'll naturally attract the right people. Remember, personal growth is a journey that is very enjoyable when you surround yourself with the right people. If, instead, you try to please everyone around, you thus compromise your personal growth and give up much of your identity. So, take risks and be you, a better and better version of yourself every day.

There are external and internal tasks and characteristics. External ones have to do with how we interact with the outside world – for example, how we communicate, solve problems, our manners, how we look at people, etc. Internal ones are all about our relationship with ourselves, what we like and do not like about ourselves, what we want to work on and improve, our emotions and how we deal with them internally, how we process and analyze our own experiences, etc. These ones are internal, and unless you make them public, they will stay as private and confidential as you want them to be. Remember, it's okay to take your time to understand these feelings of yours'. People often feel like others see through them and know all their fears, weaknesses, and doubts. What is interesting is that, at the same time, people tend to worry that others do not see their good features and characteristics as much as their bad ones. Thus, they feel like highlighting these more, often with external things and objects. We should remember that internal things are for us to realize and to work on. This internal work cannot be done by obtaining external assets. We set our own goals and tasks, and this is something that happens 'behind the curtains.' Unless, of course, you would like to share these with others. What is on the surface is a person, a member of a team and society, with their visible characteristics and characteristics that affect their interaction with others. It's important to remember that everyone has their own private struggles and aspirations, even if they seem confident. Recognizing this can help foster understanding and empathy in our relationships, as well as reduce our anxiety related to how we are perceived by others.

*Exercise:*

*Think about someone you know (choose 3 - 4 different people not related to each other).*

- *When you see them, what do you focus on?*

- *Do you analyze them and guess what issues they may be having and what they could have done better about themselves?*

- *Or do you just get a general impression read basic information, and then focus on further communication with that person?*

I bet most likely you chose the last option. Do you think you would be able to guess many things about any person? Neither would they be able to guess you. If someone wants to analyze you and make their guesses and theories, let them do it. This has nothing to do with you – the real you. As long as you do not go out with a big board in your hands where you wrote everything you have been concerned about, no one can claim anything.

When we talk about reading basic information about a person, this includes things like,

A) Is it them? This happens instantly when your brain recognizes the person.

B) Do they look alright? Is there anything weird or notable about them now?

This does not concern your socks or earrings - this is more about notable signs and changes. For example, you may have a swollen face after having cried for hours, a broken arm, or dirty clothes from crawling through the mud, or perhaps you gained or lost too much weight too quickly, and this may be related to your health, etc. The first two things we look for are more related to identifying between safety and threat – for yourself and the other individual.

C) What mood are they in today? Is there any problem I should be paying attention to? Do they need my help?

D) How should we interact today?

Of course, these are just rough outlines; you can modify these. But the idea is clear—we perceive others from different perspectives than we often think we are perceived from. Understanding this can help shift your focus from worrying about how you're seen to being more relaxed and authentic in your interactions and, therefore, enjoying them more.

Alright, now that we talked about what *they* care or do not care about, it is time to look at *you* and what *you* care or do not care about. Please ask yourself, what you would want to do and what would matter most to you in this short human lifetime in this big world. Sorry, I am not trying to make things sound gloomy; in fact, I am just aiming for the realization of the importance of our time and good choices in life. Reflecting on your values and passions can guide you toward a more fulfilling and meaningful life. Anyhow, please take a moment to think about this, and in the meantime, please let me entertain you with a story.

I was going on a vacation trip to a hot and sunny place where I could enjoy the beach, the sea, and all the wonders of summer. I was packing for it. As the owner of a rather large wardrobe, I had a difficult time choosing what items to take with me in this small suitcase. All my numerous clothing candidates looked great to me and I could easily imagine myself walking around happily and beautifully in all of these. I was going only for about ten days, but I ended up taking with me as much of my wardrobe as I could possibly fit in my suitcase after jumping on it a couple of times. How could I go without this red skirt? It would look gorgeous in the sun among those green plants, blue skies and water, and white walls along the streets! And it would be totally outrageous not to take those light pink pants that look so good with that black top that fits me so well… Anyhow, I took as much as I could and said sorry to other items that did not fit into my luggage despite all my efforts. A good thing about these efforts is that I bet they helped me burn some calories without me even noticing it as the process so absorbed me. So, I went on the trip. And then a miracle happened - I did not care what I wore there! After all those doubts and efforts, I just did not care! And the reason was simple – I was happy. I was just truly and sincerely happy there, enjoying a great time by the sea under the sun, in a beautiful place, and with good people. I enjoyed it so much that I did not want to spend extra time dressing up when I could run and take it all in during these ten days of vacation. I looked elegant with the three or four outfits I wore, and I did not even remember the rest, because my heart and mind were taken.

And this is the key – *when your heart and mind are taken* by something you love or find meaningful, your priorities adjust themselves naturally, without you having to fight yourself. You'll find that your energy flows towards what truly matters to you, making it easier to focus and take action in the right direction without being distracted by superficial things. You just naturally go where your nature is taking you. Remember when you were a kid? Maybe your mother was trying to do your hair or fix your outfit, but you were desperately trying to get done with these as soon as possible and run and play with your friends who were waiting for you outside. Well, I remember myself doing that all the time. I did not care if my little dress or shirt was ironed enough or had a tiny stain on it; I could barely care less if my pants had a tiny hole. All I cared about was to get out as soon as possible to play soccer in the street with my friends, who were already calling for me underneath my window.

### Who Cares? Social Status

I was surprised to learn that expensive brand products are mostly consumed by representatives of the middle and lower class, and people go into debt to buy these. This is often because luxury brands are seen as signs of success and help people feel like they fit in with wealthier groups. Ads and social media also make these products look like the key to a happy, successful life. Many people believe that these brands are better quality, so the cost feels more worth it. They try to signal status and pretend to be well off. By doing so, they put their social perception above their actual well-being. Well, who am I to say that you should not try to present a certain social status to others via your possessions? You do you. It is definitely not my thing, and I am not a fan of it as I see more disadvantages than advantages of it, starting with its fake and shallow nature and that it may lead to shallow and fake relationships not based on real respect and trust, and taking away from your more important areas of life to buy an illusion. I have many issues with this. But, again, who am I to tell anyone what to do? You do you.

Another argument I would like to make here is that people who actually do have the status you may want to portray often do not portray such status publicly, wear the same pair of jeans and t-shirts, and cannot be told by other people in the street. Their confidence and sense of self-worth come from within rather than from external appearances. So, once again, who cares?

## Make Peace with Imperfection

We need to allow ourselves to be imperfect and accept the fact that we all sometimes make mistakes, no matter how hard we try not to. We cannot always be at our best, and this is why it is called our best, not our normal. Recognizing our limitations helps us grow and learn from our experiences. Embracing imperfections fosters resilience and adaptability, allowing us to navigate life's challenges with greater ease. Accepting that mistakes are part of the journey encourages us to be kinder to ourselves and to appreciate our efforts rather than fixating on flaws. So, why waste your energy and time blaming and guilting yourself, and why get stressed over this? Making peace with the fact that you are far from perfect reduces the general tension and urge for instant emotional gratification as a way of consoling yourself and reducing discomfort. Being strict on yourself and being responsible is great and much better than being delusional and having an inflated ego, but at the same time, what adds to this and creates a powerful combination is accepting yourself like you would accept your best friend and giving yourself respect and support. This self-acceptance allows for personal growth without the pressure of perfection, enabling you to learn from your mistakes. When you treat yourself with kindness and understanding, it boosts your confidence and motivation, helping you pursue your goals with a healthier mindset.

Freedom to live, act, sometimes make mistakes, honesty with yourself and responsibility for your actions are a powerful trio and lead to one's focus on action-based emotional rewards much more than consumed ones. As we learn from our mistakes and work to become better, we get into an emotionally gratifying cycle of effort – improvement (achievement) – and satisfaction, which, in a way, is similar to what happens in games and makes them addictive.

We are live, changing, and dynamic creatures, and whatever characterized us at one point in time (unless we do something terrible, of course) does not stick to us forever like a label. We are what we do, and as these things change, so do we. This fluidity allows us to grow, learn, and adapt to new circumstances, making room for new experiences and insights. As soon as you allow yourself to be imperfect, something amazing happens. You become a tiny bit closer to being more perfect, a better version of yourself. Because, come on, you have just liberated yourself from all that extra pressure and effort associated with paranoid self-judgment and blame. You have released all of this energy now for better things. And maybe even have some energy left over to rest, relax, and do silly things (which, I believe, are also essential for a healthy being). This newfound freedom allows you to explore new hobbies or interests that bring you joy and fulfillment. Plus, it opens up space for meaningful connections with others as you engage more authentically and without the weight of excessive self-criticism.

You have probably heard the saying that all we do comes from two alternative sources: we act either out of love or fear. When you blame yourself for every little imperfection and every small mistake you make, you live in fear. This is a fear of mistakes, their consequences, being judged, rejected, or punished. Do you enjoy fear? Does it feel good? Does it make you confident and capable of better and smarter decisions? Does it liberate you in your actions and help you pursue your dreams? Let me guess – the answer is "Hell no!". When you accept and love yourself, others, the world, and what you do, love fills your heart and mind, leaving less room for fear. Confidence grows, you find more joy in everyday moments, and life feels more meaningful. Well, you may need some fear, just as part of survival instincts, but not more than that. So, it is like if you carried a lot of weight on your shoulders – and then it is gone! You are free. You can now move faster and easier; you have much more energy, and you are in a much better mood. Now, does this feel better? Without that weight, you're able to focus on what truly matters to you, no longer distracted by endless self-critique. Plus, you're open to new experiences and challenges that once felt overwhelming, now within reach with your lighter, refreshed mindset.

If it does feel easier and better and is so obvious, then why do we tend not to do it? The answer is we have often been raised in a belief that self-blame and punishment mean responsibility and improvement. This pattern can make us think that letting go of self-criticism means we aren't trying hard enough—when, in reality, it's often a healthier approach to lasting growth and resilience. And as decent human beings, we want to be responsible, fair, and good. In fact, these notions are the opposite. Responsibility and improvement largely come out of love. We do not want to hurt anyone because we care; we want to be good, to love, and to be loved and accepted. Therefore, we want to be responsible. Since we were kids, we have known that if we break our sibling's favorite toy, they will be very upset, and it will hurt them and may hurt the relationship we have with them. As you do not want that to happen, you better be responsible and careful with your sibling's toys. As we grow up, things, situations, and consequences become more serious, and the relationship between responsibility and caring becomes less direct. There is a stronger transactional character to our responsibility as we, for example, do what is required to not lose our jobs, or to not destroy our health, and so on. What often happens is that we develop a fear of these consequences and risks. Then, a healthy feeling of responsibility turns into a self-destructive mechanism of constant doubt and self-blame. This also happens if a kid gets punished for their mistakes in a way that fear of punishment outweighs healthy feelings and reasons. This fear can stunt personal growth as the individual becomes trapped in a cycle of overthinking and hesitancy. What would a child do in a healthy environment if he or she were to break their sibling's toy? Well, first of all, the kid would just play carefully and try not to break it. What if it happened and the toy broke? First, the kid would try to fix it, and if it is not possible, they would apologize to the sibling and see what they could do to make things better – maybe give them their toy instead, look for another toy, or look for any other possible solution. This is basically what life is or should be about. You do your best to do your best, and when – not if, but when – you mess up, you look for ways to fix things and improve, you take it as a lesson. Accepting mistakes fosters resilience, allowing you to bounce back stronger and more knowledgeable. Each setback becomes an opportunity for growth, shaping your character and enhancing your problem-solving skills. Ultimately, it's about the journey of learning and evolving through every experience, creating a more profound understanding of yourself and the world around you.

More trust in yourself, a healthier sense of judgment and responsibility, and lots of willingness to learn and improve. And with this combination, you are unstoppable. And the rewards you get are real and high-quality rewards, as you constantly set new exciting goals and reach them, and your life becomes a captivating journey. No need to hide in a shell of your fears and doubts and console yourself through consumption.

As I was writing these lines, I just realized one more thing. Right, this is exactly why we consume more when we live in fear—because action-based rewards mean that we need to do things, a lot of them, and chances of mistakes increase when you do a lot compared to when you do as little as possible and try as few new things as possible. This tendency to overconsume can serve as a temporary distraction from the anxiety associated with failure. Additionally, it creates a cycle where the comfort derived from consumption reinforces a fear of taking risks, further limiting personal growth and exploration.

In fact, our vulnerability and imperfection are, to an extent, our strengths. These make us into individuals. Alive and living people with flaws and imperfections who make mistakes, change, and improve are much more attractive and interesting to others. Imagine everyone was just perfect and correct a hundred percent of the time. How would this work? Wouldn't it make us almost the same in many ways? And with no space for learning and improvement, what would life be all about? I don't know. But when we do not grow, we stagnate or worse – degrade. Without the challenges and imperfections that come with being human, our experiences would lack depth and richness, resulting in a monotonous existence devoid of genuine connection and understanding.

## When you mess up

Yes, when, not if. We all mess up many times. When you do, do not guilt yourself much first because it is not kind. Secondly, because it is not smart, this would only enhance the bad loop of inner discomfort and all the psychological and neurological triggers and impulsive behaviors. Instead, practice self-compassion by acknowledging your mistakes as part of the human experience, which can help reduce the sting of failure. Additionally, shift your focus toward constructive actions that promote learning and growth, allowing you to move forward rather than remain stuck in a cycle of self-blame, discomfort, and search for consolation.

If a sibling or a friend came to you as they messed up or failed and were looking for your support or advice, I bet you would not roll your eyes and say, "Of course, you messed up, you stupid cow, you have always been useless, and you will always be, you worthless moron!" This way of speaking to and thinking about others is not ok, right? So why is it so common to treat ourselves differently? A key part of having a healthy relationship with yourself is treating yourself with fairness, respect, and kindness—just as you would treat others, especially your friends. At the end of the day, you are the one you spend most of your time with, right? The one who knows you most and has been through thick and thin with you – willingly or not.

## Break Away From the Context

We are too dependent on the context. When you are in an amusement park, you enjoy rides. When you are on a bus or a train, you look at it as an annoying routine. Why don't you relax and enjoy the ride? Shifting your perspective can transform ordinary moments into opportunities for enjoyment and mindfulness. By enjoying the journey rather than just focusing on the destination, you can find joy in the simple act of traveling and make the most of each experience. At the same time, listening to your favorite music, reading a book, responding to messages, etc. Yes, public transit is a super ride that allows you to do things without your stuff flying away like it would on a roller coaster; you are allowed carry-on items. And what a pleasure it is to just look outside the window and see different scenery pass by, under the sun, or while raindrops leave beautiful and peculiar traces on the window. Besides, when else would you have an opportunity to read books or do something you enjoy while not being distracted by house chores, family matters, or work? Damn, I loved my commute to work when it was about eighty minutes one way. To me, it was time for my hobbies and creativity or just to go through my favorite playlist while staring outside the train window and thinking. Those moments became a cherished part of my routine, allowing me to unwind and reflect on my day. That time helped me cultivate a sense of balance and recharge my energy before facing the demands of daily life.

We are also very dependent on context in our communication with others. It is considered normal to be social in a bar, club, or a party, but don't you dare talk to strangers on a bus. Why? Wrong context. I do not find it right and believe that this is something that restricts us and makes us feel lonelier and more disconnected. This reliance on social norms limits our opportunities to connect with others in unexpected places and enrich our lives through new friendships. And this social disconnection leads to craving more instant rewards. These are just some thoughts; you can come up with many more examples and instances where we could lift the curtain of context when you deem this appropriate and beneficial to you.

# Chapter 2. Joy of Action over Consumption

## Get off the Broken Treadmill

With our busy schedules, we barely have time to do enough of what we enjoy. We work like crazy and do a lot of what we must do to pay bills, make ends meet, and simply not be left behind. This can lead to stress and burnout, making it even harder to find time for fun. Meanwhile, our efforts need to be rewarded. Therefore, unable to go for what we really want to do on a regular basis, we go for rewards that we can get. We buy things, be it another dress, makeup kit, car, an iPhone, a can of beer, or something else. I am not talking about objects that we do need or choose to buy for a specific reason or out of a certain preference. What I am more referring to is getting something extra that you may not even need or use for the sake of having it, for that pleasure of getting it, when you feel the urge to buy and helplessly follow it. By consuming out of an urge, our daily efforts do get rewarded in a way. However, this gets us stuck in the same cycle – we need to pay more, which means that we need to work more to earn money. Working more means we need more rewards for our increasing efforts and that we have even less time to go for what we like doing (let me call these action-based rewards), which pushes us to purchase even more rewards. Congratulations, buddy – you got stuck in a cursed circle. You think you consume things, but you are also the one being consumed. It is as if you were running on that treadmill that is broken and won't stop but instead keeps accelerating.

The following diagram will represent the cycle in a much clearer way:

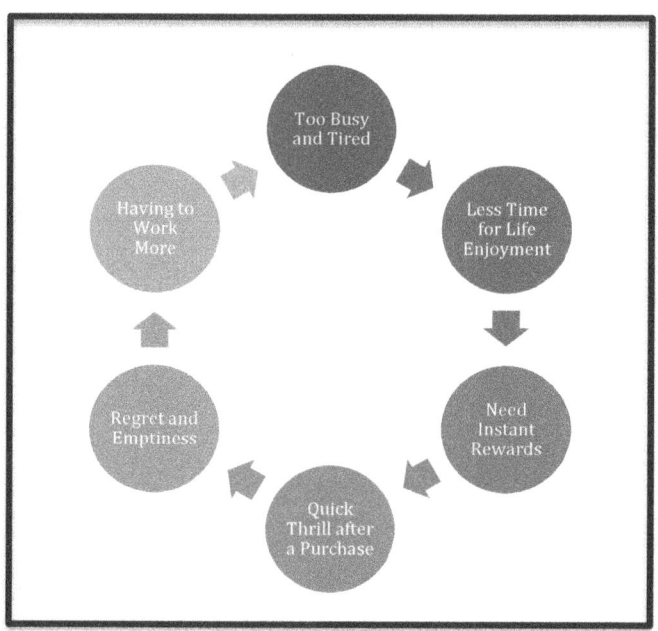

Fig. 1. Cycle of Consumption and Work

So, how can we stop this? There are several ways. Which ones would work better for you depends on your personality, character, circumstances, and preferences.

First, you can take a break from being too busy and overloaded with work, provided it is possible, of course. Maybe do less overtime work, get a less demanding and exhausting job, reduce hours, etc. You can then get yourself back together, do things you love, hang out with people you care about, and get yourself to a happier place. Do not spend much – you may want to consider moving to a cheaper apartment, cooking most of your meals, avoiding eating outside on a regular basis, and so on. Get enough rest and reset your inner gratification mechanism. Then, proceed to increase your workload gradually.

Not many of us can afford this. I definitely could not. So, another way would be forcing it. You would work even harder than you used to and focus on saving money. What happens psychologically in this case is that you have goals that you stick to. And this is something powerful that acts like an engine for us. You have a goal of saving a certain amount or for a certain thing, or you have a goal of making certain achievements at work, etc. The point is that you keep yourself motivated and rewarded on a regular basis by making realistic goals and sub-goals and reaching them step by step. Additionally, consider tracking your progress to stay motivated and reward yourself for reaching small milestones along the way.

If you simply prohibit yourself from buying more things using your will strength, you may develop healthier habits. However, here we should keep in mind that often forcing and restricting yourself acts like a time bomb, which means that at some point, you may have a short-term weakness and go crazy, do even worse than you would have if you had just continued your lifestyle the way it was. To avoid this, try to find balance by allowing yourself small, occasional treats. Also, focus on finding low-cost or free activities that bring you joy so you don't feel deprived. Nevertheless, some people do get motivated by following the rules that they set for themselves that they believe would change their lives for the better. They feel strong and respect themselves more.

In either case, what is important for this scenario is to remember that if you take something away from yourself, you should give yourself something else instead. You are a human being whose nature is to make an effort and get emotionally and physically rewarded. So, if spending hours looking for another outfit, car accessories, or bag has been supplying you with emotional gratification for a while, don't think that by taking this away from yourself, you will feel good. You need something else that would motivate you and keep you emotionally rewarded and, ideally, more than consumption used to. This could mean replacing a shopping habit with a new hobby that brings you joy, like painting or hiking, to keep your spirits high while making positive changes. Instead of the habits you seek to get rid of, you may want to incorporate more of what you enjoy doing into your life. Make time for your hobbies and meet friends regularly. Engage in activities that make you happy and spark your interest. Focus on feeling like a child again, not worrying about your outfit, but rushing to play with friends as soon as possible. It may be difficult to do with your busy schedule, but do it as much as possible and see if it works.

It is important to ensure that you cut on a specific way of getting emotional gratification but not on emotional gratification itself. When you prohibit yourself from something, then there is always an urge to do it. It is like if you starve yourself for a long time, then when you do get to the food, you will eat non-stop like a hungry wolf until you cannot take anymore. So, instead of depriving yourself of emotional rewards and starving yourself, change your diet and treat yourself to different types of emotional rewards. This could mean celebrating small achievements with activities you enjoy, like watching a favorite movie or going for a walk in nature. Additionally, consider surrounding yourself with positive people who uplift and inspire you, helping you to cultivate a healthier emotional environment.

The third option is balancing it between the two previous options. In this scenario, you take it step-by-step, gradually developing better preferences and habits while not cutting your work hours and not completely stopping the habit right away— decreasing your consumption and increasing your involvement in areas of life that you enjoy. This approach allows you to build a sustainable lifestyle that feels manageable and rewarding over time. Additionally, keep a journal to track your progress and reflect on what activities bring you the most joy, helping you stay motivated as you make changes.

Of course, there must be more ways and combinations, and you will be the best person to find what works best for you. My goal is to give you some ideas and encourage you to think in the right direction – your good knowledge of yourself and your situation, as well as your creativity, will do the rest.

Have you noticed that very active people tend to shop less? And vice versa. My friends who have lives full of captivating activities wear the same shirts for years and use the same old backpack until it is so worn out that it cannot be used anymore. For them, active rewards are enough to keep them satisfied and happy, and they do not want to exchange their fun times for something material.

## From Having Time to Making Time

Have you heard that saying that if you really want something, you will find time, while if you do not want it, you will find an excuse? Another version of it is that you will 'make' time. And there is a crucial difference between the mindset of making time and having time. When you think of yourself as having or not having time for something, you take a passive role, while when you make time for people and things that you want in your life, you are an active constructor of your present – which also means of your future.

Of course, we do not possess magic superpowers and cannot create time out of nothing. But we can try to be as efficient and creative with time as possible. It is like the game of Tetris where you are to fit as many blocks of different shapes as possible by rotating and moving them around. You can do something similar with your time. By prioritizing tasks,  focusing on what truly matters, moving different activities to different time slots, and reorganizing them, you can use time much more efficiently – and this means you will be getting more action-based rewards, resulting from achievements, completing things you need to do, and enjoying things you love.

This concept will also help you look at your time as something you have a significant amount of control over. Your healthy responsibility and positive motivation will increase, and you will start doing better at filling your time with things that matter to you. By recognizing your ability to manage your schedule, you can reduce stress and make more intentional choices about how you spend your days. Additionally, regularly reviewing and adjusting your priorities can keep you aligned with your goals and values, ensuring that your time is spent in ways that truly enrich your life.

## From Having to Doing

Think of your childhood. What were your favorite toys as a kid? Ones that you could just have and play with - like toy cars, dolls, or stuffed animals, or ones that were intended for you to build things – like LEGO and puzzles? For me, it was the latter type of toy that I preferred playing with. I was quite attached to my stuffed toys, including my very much-loved stuffed elephant, Sloniha, which I, at an early age, claimed to be my daughter. I would carry *Sloniha* and have her sit next to me, as a proud and caring elephant Mom should, but there was something very entertaining about those constructors, puzzles, and other toys that suggested thinking and action.

My elephant offspring have long grown up and taken off; I think she moved to another proud little elephant Mom, but my preference for action-based mental and emotional gratification stayed on. I find that making and doing things can be a never-ending source of inspiration because there will always be things to do and to make in life, and we can always look for ways to do them better or differently. Now, I am not saying we should all be making clothes and furniture for ourselves – this would be way too challenging – but we can focus on things we can do rather than things we can have. Engaging in creative projects or hands-on activities can foster a sense of accomplishment and joy, reminding us of the value in the process rather than just the result.

## Action-Based Gifts

The topic of activities brings me to my most recent view on gifts. We often do not know what to give people for Christmas, birthdays, or other occasions. Everyone seems to mostly have what they need, or we just don't really know what they need. So, we often end up giving each other things that we do not really use. How about action-based gifts? Like an invitation or a ticket to an activity or event, membership, or a gift card for a certain activity club or a store with things they would use for their hobbies? These may not only be pleasant and useful but may also inspire and push the person to actually do more and grow. Plus, such gifts create opportunities for shared experiences, allowing you to bond with the recipient while encouraging them to explore their interests and passions.

If you think of the massive consumption that happens during the holiday season – Christmas shopping being the top example – there are billions of items bought as presents every day all over the world intending to demonstrate to someone you care about them and wish them a happy holiday. At the same time, it is a present they likely will never use. We often do not know each other well enough to guess what exactly they may want and need, and these days, everything is rather easy to find, so people usually have what they need. Instead of adding to the clutter, we could focus on giving meaningful experiences or thoughtful gestures that truly resonate, making the holidays more memorable and personal for everyone involved. I remember spending hours looking for gifts for family and friends and often failing to get them something they would really need. Then I had to decide to switch to gift cards, movie tickets, beautician services, or, for my outdoor friends, a gift card selling outdoor equipment. This way, if you have a general idea of a person's hobbies, you can be sure your gift will be used and not collect dust for years in all the apartments they move to. It is difficult for many people, including myself, to get rid of things that have been given as a gift.

## Use Your Sense of Achievement

As I listen to audiobooks on Audible during my night-time baby feeds, I keep earning badges – for the number of books I listened to, the number of different genres, length, etc. While these badges do not mean any extra credit and do not have any practical value, I caught myself checking on whether I received more badges. We enjoy these little awards we get, don't we? We enjoy that sense of accomplishment coming with some kind of external acknowledgment or expression of these. This highlights the importance of recognizing and celebrating small milestones in our lives, as they can boost our motivation and encourage us to keep striving for more. Creating checklists for yourself for different to-do items and then checking those boxes can be a very pleasant activity, especially for those of us who are more visual. It is not only pleasant but triggers those dopamine pathways – of anticipated reward (when you are creating the list and drawing the boxes) and accomplishment (when you check the boxes). I noticed that when I do this, I tend to look much less for dopamine through stuff, snacks, mindless scrolling online, playing games, etc. By finding joy in these small achievements, I create a healthier feedback loop that fulfills my need for satisfaction and keeps me more focused on my goals rather than seeking instant gratification from less meaningful sources.

## From Self-Pity to Responsibility

I think that each of us could admit that we could do better at a number of things and that there is always space for improvement. If you admit your mistakes and weaknesses, what it does is that it opens your eyes to reality and ways to make things better, to different perspectives and lessons. More than that, it empowers you. How? You see the consequences of your mess-ups, and you realize that you are the one in charge of many things in your life, the one who defines how your life will be. See, it works both ways – if your mess-ups tend to play a negative role in your current reality, then your work on improvement will have a big positive impact. This way, taking responsibility for your actions puts you in charge of what you do and say and, as a result, much of what will be happening in your life. And this realization is life-changing. It's a powerful step towards growth.

Say you are not happy with how you behave in certain situations, with your social skills, or any other skills, your sense of style, shape, posture, way of life – or pretty much anything else that you can make changes to. This does not define you forever, not at all. You can act, which means that you can change. Growth happens through effort and intention. Every small change adds up to a new version of yourself.

## Use a trick or two that helps.

Try not to think about an elephant. Try really hard not to think about an elephant. I bet all you are thinking about right now is an elephant. The same happens when you pity yourself. You have something that makes you feel bad. You want to get away from it, resolve it, and move to something better — at least, this would be something normal to want in this situation. And then you pity yourself, and you do it very diligently. You remind yourself about all this negativity you are trying to get away from. But dwelling on it keeps you stuck in the same place. True change starts when you focus on the solution, not the problem. Constantly pitying yourself and putting yourself in the position of a victim brings you the opposite of the empowerment you get from taking responsibility because you make a helpless victim out of yourself and often focus on the fact or illusion that this was not your fault – which means this is something that does not depend on you – instead of taking full or partial responsibility and proceeding to solutions.

Another thing that helps is imagining yourself in the third person or as a computer game character. Look at this creature and say to yourself that you may be anything else but a person who miserably gives up. That no matter what, you will go on with dignity and grace. Whatever you would like to include in the menu, this is your character and your life. This trick will cheer you up and give you more confidence. Besides the game component of it – imagining yourself as a game character – it makes it more interesting, gives you a better sense of responsibility, control, and empowerment, and will help bring you closer to that good effort-reward relationship that is the foundation of games. This perspective shifts challenges into opportunities for growth. And it helps you stay focused on progress rather than setbacks. Please don't overdo it, though. Or it would border with delusion, main character syndrome, and all other goodies that you don't want to happen. As you get stronger and start feeling better, your challenges will be kinder to you and dearer to your heart, and that big problematic elephant that you have been thinking and suffering about, deprived of your attention, will become smaller and smaller and will then disappear behind the horizon. Again, do not get too caught up in this, as I assume you would not want to fall into a swamp of delusion. Know limits and get reality checks, will you? Growth is gradual, and it's important to keep a grounded perspective. Remember, facing challenges with a clear mind leads to lasting progress, not just temporary relief.

## Take ownership of your actions and life.

It may be a part of human nature to pity ourselves – it may be one of our instruments of self-defense and stress reduction — this denial and emotional discharge. It's okay. But hey, how about this: take one day to pity yourself with no shame or self-blame. Eat all the treats you want, watch all the movies you please, cry like a three-year-old, and complain like a professional complainer – do it diligently and fully until you are sick of it. Get enough sleep to rest like you did when you were four and were sent to bed, which, of course, back then you hated but now secretly miss. And then, get yourself back together, take responsibility, and act on problem resolution. Indulgence can be a temporary release, but it's action that brings lasting change. The key is to balance self-care with personal growth, knowing when to pause and when to move forward.

Remember that your thoughts become your reality. They influence your reality a lot and determine how you feel and act at a certain moment. Sometimes, some painful experience just keeps haunting us, and we cannot get it out of our heads. I remember one of those times when I was extremely upset about something and felt ruined and stuck. My brother gave me a very good idea of how to not think about it. Every time a thought about that subject crossed my mind, I was to replace it with another one – be it an image of a black screen, a monkey, thoughts of what my plan was for the day, or anything else. It is a conscious replacement, which means you are aware of it. It helps. And it can also make you more productive and even entertained. Guess what? If you keep yourself busy, you will have less space available in your mind to think about what bothers you, and your misery will have no choice but to be replaced bit by bit with other thoughts and emotions. This shift in focus can bring a sense of relief and control. Staying engaged with positive, or just necessary, tasks fuels momentum, turning small actions into significant progress.

## Make Yourself, Do Not Imagine Yourself

It is difficult to overestimate the importance of self-image in one's life. And who would be a better fit to see how it changes people's lives than a successful plastic surgeon? Especially if this plastic surgeon helped people improve what they considered major defects in their appearance around the middle of the 20th century, long before plastic surgery became a very common thing and a go-to for any minor change. The successful plastic surgeon I am talking about was Maxwell Maltz, who later wrote his famous and ground-breaking book Psycho-Cybernetics, where he stated that an individual's self-image acts as a blueprint for their life. This self-perception dictates what a person believes they can or cannot achieve, therefore expanding or limiting one's abilities and opportunities. He states that an improvement in one's self-image can lead to improvements in their performance and overall well-being. By self-image, he means not only physical appearance but an overall self-perception as it relates to many aspects and areas.

As mentioned in the previous section, we often try to improve our self-image through consumption and other means while avoiding the actual work and failing to actually make a change in ourselves so that our self-image and our real image align. It is important to know who you are and who you want to be in order to determine how to get there.

## V - Main Character Syndrome

One of the times I was an extra in movies, I remember there was that fellow extra guy who, on his first day in the background, would not stop talking about how this was the beginning of his great career in film, which was causing mixed feelings of amusement and annoyance among us. I bet in his imagination, he was already a renowned actor giving interviews to major networks. All while sitting in the crowd of other extras wearing a mask that conceals his face and serves the mere purpose of being one little piece of the environment for the major action. Not to undermine the importance of background performers at all, our purpose was to help create the environment around us. He did not understand his role but instead tried as hard as possible to jump in front of the camera where he could. This is the worst that an extra can do and can result in everyone having to reshoot the scene or, if needed, in that extra removal from the set. It was annoying and comical for us, as there would be stuntmen imitating a fight and dramatically falling on the mats when, in the midst of that, he would 'accidentally' squeeze in his masked face somewhere or get so over the board with his cheering that one would think he was on some kind of mushrooms or something. In his mind, he was the main character of his own imaginary movie.

Main character syndrome is something that has recently been talked about a lot. This is attention-seeking behavior that is even more inappropriate as the person tries to be a 'main character' in a situation where they are definitely not. It is trying to make things about yourself somewhere where something much more significant is happening to someone else. It undermines the importance of others' experiences and can create an imbalance in relationships. True empathy and connection come from being present and supportive, not trying to steal the spotlight.

The truth is we all have roles in different circumstances, and understanding your role at any specific moment is the healthiest thing. If your friend fell and broke something, you would not, I assume, try to make the situation about yourself, would you? Your role in the moment would be that of a helper focusing on your friend. Being aware of your role helps maintain harmony and respect in relationships. It allows you to show up with the right energy for the situation without overshadowing others. Embracing your role also deepens your sense of purpose, giving you clarity and emotional balance. It also strengthens your realistic and healthy perception of self, contributing to good and healthy self-esteem without the need to prove anything to anyone or escape into the realm of delusion.

Main character syndrome is also associated with imagining yourself as the main character of an imaginary movie and acting as such. Have you ever cringed at someone speaking in a third person about themselves? I certainly did. This feels so unnatural and self-absorbed. But ok, let's say someone is imagining a movie where they are the main character. You still do not get it right from the cinematography perspective, even if you are always the main character everywhere. Come on, have you ever seen a movie where the main character is always at the center of attention? How about scenes where he or she is just a passerby witnessing some event? In that specific moment, their role is that of a witness or passerby. In another scene, they may be assisting someone else with a task or something of that sort. We all have different roles in different moments, and this is what keeps us all and the world around us going.

Years ago, I taught kindergarten kids in China English. Groups varied in age from about 1–2-year-olds to 6-7. We used to play games with the kids when learning, and this was an amazing experience. I remember one of the older groups was learning animal vocabulary, and we were to enact a little play with different animals. When distributing roles, I was faced with the fact that everyone wanted to be a tiger, a highly respected animal in China. Well, you can guess how this one would go – a bunch of tigers, all wanting to dominate the forest. Of course, not everyone got to be a tiger on that day. We did end up having monkeys, rabbits, and other animals as well. And this made the play possible and meaningful. Each role, no matter how different or small, adds value to the bigger picture. Understanding that every part is essential to foster collaboration and harmony, as well as a healthy perception of self.

Ok, you can say, cool, but what does this have to do with our topic here? Well, guess what – the more dissatisfied you are with your life or the more stressed you are, for one reason or another, or the more your self-image differs from your real self, the more you are inclined to seek instant gratification and shortcuts. You could also try to protect that imaginary self-image by buying things and accessories instead of looking into the core of the problem. As I mentioned before, in this book, my goal is to look into many kinds of diverse possible triggers and reasons for excessive consumption so that each of my dear readers hopefully find some that would relate to them. By exploring these different angles, I aim to offer insights that can lead to meaningful self-reflection and positive change.

## V - Self-Importance through Misery

It was a sunny spring morning in Richmond, British Columbia. I was an extra in one of the TV series that was being shot there. The scene was being shot by the water under the sun, and the lovely scent of the fresh breeze was pleasant and inspiring. Our role was easy – we were to just sit at the restaurant pretending to casually chat with each other and sip on our beverages. All while enjoying the lovely sunny spring day and getting paid for it. Around the corner, there was what is called background holding, which is a room or a tent where background members kept their belongings and hung out between the times when they were required on set. Right by it, there was another tent where snacks, fruits, and beverages were placed for everyone to enjoy. In between being on set, we could do whatever we pleased in the holding – chat with each other, read books, eat, or do our own projects. All while being paid. If this does not sound like a nice and pretty easy hustle for you, I don't know what does. It's the perfect balance of work and relaxation, allowing for both productivity and leisure. Don't get me wrong; there were days when you would be spending long hours in the cold, in an uncomfortable outfit of some kind of ancient servant in a corset or shoes that hurt, with little food and far away from any public transit. But overall, I think we can agree that the job of an extra is not one of the most demanding ones and is definitely very entertaining.

So, here we were, sitting at the tables under the sun, with the nice blue water in front of our eyes, pretending to have engaging conversations with each other while silently moving our lips and making different facial expressions. And then the movie crew said, "Background performers, thank you. Please go back to the holding until we call you." The guy sitting opposite me exhaled loudly and, with a tired expression, mumbled, "Again... We've been here for hours... I'm working so hard." I could not help but stare at him. I mean, after 'performing' hard, we were sent right across the corner to hang out hard and eat hard in the holding, or maybe to listen to the music or read hard. Life is hard, isn't it? I think I even could not resist saying to him that for a diversity of experience he may want to try working long hours on a construction site instead and see how he would like that. Was I a bit of a jerk? Maybe. But the guy did not complain after, and the peaceful harmony of the spring day was restored, at least for the ones around him.

I bet we have all seen people complain and be miserable, talk continuously about having it hard, and seem to derive some kind of weird pleasure from it. There is a difference in behavior if you compare that where someone complains and then looks for a solution and that where the person is not interested in any solutions but secretly finds pleasure in complaining, almost making it their whole lifestyle. In my observation, this is often to add significance to one's persona by portraying their work to be harder and more important than it actually is. This type of behavior can create an illusion of importance, but it often masks insecurity or fear of inadequacy. By constantly focusing on the struggle, they avoid taking responsibility or seeking personal growth, staying stuck in a cycle of self-victimization.

### V - Real Action Happens Behind the Scenes

While the two above-mentioned people dreamt of big self-importance, one through seeking an inappropriate level of attention and giving in to the main character syndrome and the other through acting out misery, there were ones who were doing the actual hard work but were barely seen or heard. These were movie crew members who did all kinds of set work, video, audio, costume, and other kinds of work that were crucial for a movie or series to come to life. The real action, apart from the one coming from actors, was largely happening behind the scenes. Their dedication and skill often go unnoticed, but they are the backbone that supports the entire production.

So does self-improvement. Most of it happens behind the scenes and away from delusional self-image or self-pity, without seeking attention or affirmation of one's importance. It happens through work on yourself, on your areas of improvement – be it a healthy diet and a good workout routine, educating yourself on certain subjects, or working through certain psychological issues or behavior patterns – you name it. It has little to do with imagining yourself but everything to do with making yourself into who you want to become.

## Beware of Culture of Milestones

As I was standing in line at the bank waiting for the next customer service representative to become available, I was looking at the big screen where they were playing their ads and promoting their new types of accounts, credit lines, and cards. These were linked to certain milestones in people's lives – getting a student loan, a car loan, getting married, getting a mortgage, having a baby, retiring, etc. We live in a culture of milestones, from one big event in our lives to another. How about what is in between? What happens in between is life itself, while these milestones accelerate our lives. There are people in their 30s looking forward to retirement! And not just planning their retirement but actually *looking forward* to it! How about the 30-40 years in between? Aren't you just rushing through your life – that is already short enough? The moments in between are where true growth and experiences happen. By focusing only on the future, you risk missing out on the richness of the present.

You may have noticed in the list of milestones I mentioned above a word that repeats itself awkwardly and too much – getting. Milestones are often associated with getting something. You got a car, or a smartphone, or a home – excellent, you need these. But these are merely instruments in your life. A car helps you travel around, a phone these days is something almost totally essential for communication. Also, it performs as a computer, and a home is – I know this is getting awkward, as it is too obvious – something you live in. These are there for you to live a better life and not the other way around. You are not there to just serve as a tool to get these objects and reach these milestones.

I notice that earning and spending money is a measure of success in society. Look, I am now earning this much! Look, I bought myself this! I can spend this much! It is so expensive, but I can afford it – which translates to 'I am important, meaningful, and respected.' What happens here is a substitution. Usually, your life feels meaningful when you do or feel something important to you. There is nothing wrong with obtaining material goods that you want but these are short-term joys and cannot replace your deeper relationship with yourself and the world. True fulfillment comes from connection, growth, and meaning, not just possessions. Besides, consumption creates more milestones in your life, and between them, there is a vacuum – little motivation other than looking forward to the next milestone. Living from A to B, from weekend to weekend, vacation to vacation, and purchase-to-purchase takes from you huge junks of your life that you could be enjoying. Interestingly, while there are many more opportunities for people in developed countries to chase their dreams, people in the first world often have a sense of entitlement that makes us focus on what we deserve to have rather than what we want to do and feel, which enforces the material and consumption aspect of milestones. This mindset shifts our focus from personal growth and fulfillment to external validation and accumulation.

This is why if you appreciate every moment, you will feel that material goods will lose a lot of their meaning. You will start seeing things differently, as processes, not milestones, as doing, not getting. This shift in perspective opens you up to a deeper sense of contentment and fulfillment rooted in experiences rather than possessions.

Now, don't get me wrong - we do need a home, a vehicle, and many other things. And there is nothing wrong with wanting things for yourself or your family. It is natural and overall beneficial. In my opinion, the problem appears when these material milestones take up the vast majority of space between your ears and cloud your perception of life taking away your ability to see and live life in between them.

## From Extrinsic to Intrinsic Rewards

Most of what was mentioned in this chapter has to do with moving more toward intrinsic rewards as compared to extrinsic ones. Intrinsic rewards come from within you and are related to such things as your own goals, sense of accomplishment, self-improvement, learning and activities you enjoy or find fulfilling. These are longer-lasting rewards and boost your sense of satisfaction, motivation, and creativity. Motivation and creativity, in turn, help you pursue more activities, leading to intrinsic rewards. This creates a positive cycle where each success fuels the next, reinforcing personal growth and fulfillment.

In turn, extrinsic rewards are ones coming from outside and can be praise and recognition by others, monetary and material rewards. These, while often more instant and straightforward and definitely still essential for us in many ways, do not have as much of a strong, lasting effect and, instead of motivating you, put you in a dependency loop. Relying too much on external validation can lead to a sense of emptiness when those rewards are not available. True fulfillment comes from internal growth, where the drive and satisfaction are rooted in your values and achievements, not in external feedback.

Fig. 2. Example of Intrinsic vs Extrinsic Rewards at the Workplace

# Chapter 3. Money-Saving Powers of Your Mood and Attitude

## Let's Play - a Perfect Balance

*"We don't stop playing games because we grow old; we grow old because we stop playing games."*

*– Bernard Shaw.*

I remember when I was a kid and a teenager, I used to be terrified of dentists. And it made sense – I used to have many cavities and a very big sensitivity to pain, which could often not be taken away even after a double dose of anesthesia.

I would have nightmares the night before; I would often feel sick in the morning – my body was scared of each dentist trip and tried to find ways to escape. I remember the moments when I was out of the dentist's office, exhausted, often in pain, and craving something that would console me and make me happy. And what I wanted most at those moments was usually to eat something tasty or to buy something nice. And I still remember how, after one of such trips, Mom bought us our first or second computer game – Pharaoh and Cleopatra, a strategy where you were a ruler of Egypt and had a number of missions where you were to build a prospering city and fight its enemies. I loved it, and I still do to this day. And you know, I have noticed that I crave to play it during those moments of my life when I am overwhelmed with stress and feel helpless and unable to solve some of my real-life issues. Then I can take an hour to be a Pharaoh while sitting comfortably in my chair and enjoying some treats, with no stress, and build a whole city while receiving flattering notifications on the screen saying how so-and-so thinks I am a great ruler – a process full of little challenges and rewards, something that is often missing in an overwhelmingly stressful life.

Now, you may ask me, this all makes sense, but what do I do with this? We all, from time to time, get very stressed and exhausted. Is there a cure for that? No – if you mean a magic remedy that will take all your future stress away from your life; yes – if you mean a way to deal with it more efficiently and with less damage. The key is to find something useful and pleasant that, at the same time, can be broken down into little steps and challenges that you can resolve with little effort and fast emotional reward, bringing into action those short dopamine paths. And don't forget that consistency matters: by regularly practicing these small, manageable tasks, you build a foundation that helps reduce the intensity of stress over time.

What we love about games – not only computer games but games in general - is that there is always a result, and people's favorite games have quicker results. There must be a balance – if the game is too easy and you get rewarded before putting in any real effort, you may get bored. On the other hand, if you spend an hour trying to figure out that labyrinth or finding a way to fight that one annoying little green monster who just has more powers than you no matter what, then you may as well just give up and do something else. You may have had enough problems and concerns already to let yourself suffer even more misery from this freaky little monster. The monster has to resist and challenge you until it gets on your nerves, but then, soon enough, it makes a weird sound and explodes, opening a new level with new monsters to defeat.

And this is the key reason why games are so addictive – it is a constant sequence of challenges and rewards. After each challenge, there is a reward, and after each reward, you look forward to a new challenge. Why? Because you know there will be a reward and you are curious and excited about it. Additionally and importantly, the anticipation of a reward and knowing when exactly it will come and in what shape triggers dopamine release even more than getting the reward itself. You tell yourself that you will only play one more time or until the next level, but once you get the award, the new challenge appears immediately and carries you away, along with all of your excitement for the next award and next challenge, and so on.

Now, if we can be Pharaohs and warriors sitting in our chairs in a room and sipping on soda, why do we not try creating a strong emotional drive for us in our own lives? Is it possible? Look, these are the facts: you have had and will always have challenges in life, no matter what. You may want to try to escape and hide from them, or you can embrace them and take all you can out of them. See, the key difference here is that in a game, we are safe – we either win and get rewarded, or a virtual green monster kills our character, we get upset, eat another cookie, and play again, and maybe again, until we win, or just forget about it and move on with our day. In real life, it is different. Your character is you, and risks and hurts are real. You have more to lose but also much more to win. So, if you create an environment for yourself where you take the situations you have in life, break them down into tasks and challenges, and go solve them one by one – don't forget to reward yourself with something you truly enjoy – then your love for life will grow, and so will your skills and chances to have a better reality, and then you will start getting more action-based high-quality rewards and will search much less for stuff and consumption-based rewards. Over time, this shift will not only improve your mindset but also boost your resilience, making it easier to handle life's challenges with a sense of confidence and accomplishment.

To be clear with you, I have nothing against computer games – it is everyone's own choice, and in many cases, it can even help develop your brain. What I am concerned with is when people use games as an escape from their reality, as a substitution, and when they are not happy in life. This is what should be targeted and worked on. Otherwise, we all may want to be a Pharaoh for an hour or two, or a warrior, or a pilot, or whatever else the game world can offer us.

Let's play. And let's play in real life. How many times per day have we presented a challenge and are taking it as a problem and stressed out over it? Why don't we take every possible opportunity to play and approach problems with curiosity and some excitement, thereby involving "healthy" adrenaline? Let's say you are on a bus or train every day in the morning and evening on your way to and from work. And because, of course, you are not alone in this, often all seats are taken, and you end up standing on your feet. And as if it was not annoying enough, guess what? All things you can hold on to are also taken. Damn it! Well then, when it happens to me, I take a second to be annoyed, and after that, I play. I take the challenge of not holding on to anything at all and balancing on my feet the way I would if I were skiing, snowboarding, or surfing. I bend my knees a little bit and start feeling and responding to every little movement that the bus or train makes. I cannot say that at moments like this, I feel the way I did when surfing in Costa Rica or skiing in Europe or Canada, but I definitely feel much better than I would if I were miserably complaining to myself all the way about how inconvenient and tiring it is. And this is because I feel playful – there appears a game, even if just a little one, in my life, and a game means that you will have a sequence of little challenges and rewards. Indeed, when the bus suddenly stops, and people who are holding on to something are almost flying away, I remain on my feet the way I was, as if I were taking a somewhat more difficult slope or wave this time – and I feel great. Sometimes, I also fly a meter or so, like a lid from a wine bottle, but this makes it fun as I just keep a score in my head. Or let's say you come back home exhausted after work, but you still need to do the dishes. Why not time yourself and see how fast you can do it?

It's about finding joy in the unexpected, turning even the smallest disruptions into playful challenges that make life feel more dynamic and less predictable. Over time, this mindset builds a sense of light-heartedness, where you can face even more intense moments with a calm and confident approach, knowing that you can always adapt and enjoy the game.

Another reason why playfulness is great is because it can give you many funny and unusual moments to remember in the future. Let's say you or your buddy failed. There was an awkward or hilarious situation that will give you laughs for a long time afterward, and you will feel rewarded again and again just by remembering this experience. For example, you fall, or, as it happened with one of my buddies on a bus, you do not react in time to a sudden turn, make an abrupt move, and your shoe flies off and lands on someone's newspaper, or even worse, on a driver's wheel. And then you jump in one shoe all the way from the back of the bus, saying 'Excuse me' to everyone and apologizing to the driver while hoping they do not notice that your sock has a big hole in it. That's something you could later laugh at with your friends over and over again.

Going back to chemistry, there is also something about laughter and about playing in general. This helps release happy hormones in our brains and makes us healthier, physically and mentally, while also rewarding us emotionally and motivating us. As a kindergarten school teacher and a student services coordinator in the past, I have always included game components in the study process. Especially during long study hours, people tend to lose attention and interest in any subject – especially if it is not something strikingly interesting – and I do not sincerely think that learning theory about business and hospitality is interesting enough to maintain motivation for eight hours straight. Our human body is simply not designed to be seated and focused on one thing for more than a certain amount of time. Some believe it is around one hour, while others claim it to be no more than 20 minutes in order for you to stay focused and efficient. That's why incorporating short breaks and varying activities into your study routine can refresh your mind, allowing you to come back to the task with renewed focus and energy rather than forcing yourself to push through the fatigue.

So, at one of my past jobs, in addition to regular breaks, I often asked instructors to let me know when the class seemed tired and absent-minded. At that time, I would come in for a few minutes, and we would play some games that required movement or a high amount of emotional or intellectual involvement – a fun type, not a boring theory of concepts or some other concepts for the sake of more concepts. Some days, we played charades and musical chairs, and it was a lot of fun. I could observe how much stress and fear students had accumulated in their bodies – they would sit in the chair every five seconds as they were afraid to lose, and I would have to encourage them to keep running until I stopped the music. By the end of the game, they were much more relaxed and happier and would run and laugh all the time until the music stopped. When the students continued with their class after the game, they were much more productive. I also made my Spanish language student do squats after wrong responses as he had mentioned to me that he also wanted to get into a better shape. These were one-on-one classes, of course; otherwise, making only one student do that out of the whole class would be somewhat weird.

We do not notice how much stress, tension, and fear we accumulate in our bodies. Playing– all different types of playing – helps break these chains and resets us, if not to the original liberated state, then at least pretty close to it. Playing releases in us a fun and creative energy, which is opposite to what drugs us into self-destructive behaviors. It shifts our focus away from worries and negative patterns, creating space for joy and spontaneity. Over time, incorporating more play into your life can act as a powerful tool for emotional release, reducing stress and promoting a healthier, more balanced outlook on life.

## Humor on Guard of Your Credit Card

Humor is one of the key components of happiness. It reduces levels of stress and anxiety, increases motivation, and enhances learning. Without humor, all of our challenges and problems would be stressful nightmares, and difficult episodes of our lives would be endless, bitter sensations. Humor is one of our defense mechanisms that protect our mental stability and, as a result, our health as well. Maybe this is why, as I noticed, people who grew up in similarly challenging conditions, even if they are from different parts of the world, tend to have a similar sense of humor. Humor also creates a sense of connection, allowing us to bond over shared experiences and find lightness in even the toughest situations, fostering resilience and a sense of community.

Let more humor into your life and look at some annoying things as funny. You will be much better off emotionally and physically, and you will be getting emotional rewards even from something that was supposed to tire and stress you out. Therefore, you would crave less instant gratification from consumption.

I used to work in Customer Service at a call center, where I assisted our clients by phone and email in the four languages I speak. Many of my calls were about technical difficulties – this is what people normally call customer service for. They would obviously not call you just to find out how your cat is doing or to tell you that they love your services - although there was once a customer who called us on Christmas evening just to wish us a Merry Christmas—God bless that person, really. So, people were calling because they had some technical difficulties, and while most of the time, these were easy to solve, sometimes there were more difficult and time-consuming issues. And the ways people reacted to those were very different. No need to tell you that we had customers yell at us every single day and every hour, and there was even no need to worry as their problem could be resolved in one minute. It felt bad to us, and I must admit that sometimes we even cried after being called names for something that was not our fault and often not being heard when you already provided the answer and solution. I remember being told by a customer that although she had never met or seen me, I must be a stupid ugly b*tch. This was because the lady forgot her password, and the "stupid system" was not letting her in. Cool. It felt terrible to me. And I was mad at her. But it also must have been terrible for the customer. Imagine how much stress they must have gone through before they decided to pick up their phone, call us, and pour it all on an agent's head. And this is unfortunate.

There was also another type of customer. These were people laughing at problems, even when the issue was indeed on our side. They were friendlier and much more understanding. They would make jokes and sincerely laugh at them. They could participate in problem-solving much more efficiently than those who chose to take the role of a furious victim unwilling to listen to anything or anyone. I am talking about choosing a role because I believe that it is always our conscious choice to act a certain way, even if we make this choice in a matter of seconds and we do not notice when the choice is made. We still make a choice — we choose to stop or not stop a certain type of behavior. So, let's say two ladies, A and B have been entering their passwords – that they believed were correct – but the system was not letting them in. Lady A chose to stress out over this fact, yelling at a number of customer service representatives and managers, escalating the call from one to another, probably losing a bunch of calories while doing it and helping those people she yelled at lose some calories as well—and guess what, the stupid system still would not let her in! Because the system does not care. It does not care if you diligently yelled at everyone in the office, one by one, if you carefully chose the worst names you could give them if you promised to go to court with this issue, and if you ran out of breath while doing all of this. The system essentially does not even care whether you are right or wrong – if it does not work, then it just does not work, and you should then look for a different solution. Lady B, on the other hand, would first confirm whether there is really no way to get the system to accept the password. Once this is confirmed, she would say, well, that is strange that the system is now not accepting her correct password anymore, but what can she do. She may laugh at the fact that even machines get old and lose their memory or that even a computer does not want to collaborate with her on such a difficult day. And she would proceed to a solution, which is taking her notebook, composing a new password, and changing it. A couple of minutes and this is done. Little stress and even some emotional rewards – the satisfaction of a completed task combined with some laughing and positive, friendly interaction.

Now, which of these people do you think may need consolation and an instant reward after this issue? Lady A, who had a totally stressful and negative experience – and let's be honest, made it a totally stressful and negative experience for herself, for she had a choice. There are different situations and problems, and sometimes things are simply terrible. However, in most cases, remember that you have a choice to make your experience less negative, neutral, or even more positive than negative. And, as we saw from previous sections, stress causes more of an urge for instant rewards, while a happier life filled with positive emotions and favorite activities makes these unnecessary. By actively choosing a positive or neutral perspective, you build resilience and gradually train your mind to seek solutions rather than focus on frustrations, making it easier to maintain well-being even during tough times.

So far, my champion customer was a lovely lady who I spent one hour with on the phone and who was making me laugh all the time until my stomach was hurting, and my head was helplessly jumping on the table. Nothing was working for her, and she laughed at that very much and very contagiously. When something started working, she laughed even more because it felt funny to her that now it worked. She was finding a positive experience in both successful and unsuccessful steps. She laughed at my name in a very funny way; she laughed at the temporary password she was given, at the picture on the screen, and at everything she could. And I could not resist laughing either. My neighboring agents and supervisors were giving me strange looks and wondering what was going on with me. Some of them told me later that they were jealous I had such an adorable and funny customer on the phone while others were being yelled at. I bet both of us, the lovely lady on the phone and myself, got a good amount of dopamine for the day and left the phone as stronger and happier people. Moments like these remind us that finding humor in everyday struggles can make a huge difference, not only in our mood but also in creating a positive ripple effect for those around us.

Apart from making you generally happier and allowing for less stress and tension, which reduces your craving for instant gratification through consumption, humor also helps you stay away from unnecessary spending in a more direct way. When you are willing to laugh at yourself and your situation, you are less likely to want to prove anything to yourself or others. You are then less likely to go out of your way to chase brands or buy items you do not need in order to maintain a certain image. Last but not least, by reducing the levels of stress and anxiety and increasing motivation, humor decreases our urge for compulsive behaviors and consumption on a neurological level. Humor also encourages a more mindful approach to life, helping you appreciate what you have rather than constantly seeking new, unnecessary material possessions.

## From Stress to Challenge

Our lives are full of stress. We get plenty of it daily - at our jobs, schools, homes, and outside. Positive stress, if I may refer to it so, just for the simplicity of it, is related to change and improvement and gives you a good portion of excitement. It is something that encourages you and brings you to a better self. This is something that a runner feels before a race, a dancer at the last rehearsal before the performance and at the performance itself, or a painter finishing some challenging details. It can be anything. It is different from stress in that negative meaning we are used to because it includes excitement and motivates action. Positive stress can also arise when you're learning a new skill or stepping out of your comfort zone, like delivering a speech or trying an adventurous hobby. Similarly, it shows up when you tackle a difficult problem, like solving a puzzle or overcoming a work-related challenge, and feel that sense of accomplishment when you succeed.

Stress, in its negative meaning, often occurs when a situation or outcome does not depend on us, and we find ourselves helpless - completely or partially. Another difference is that a challenge often ends with a reward and moral satisfaction, while stress, in the best-case scenario, can end with relief. It often leaves us feeling drained rather than fulfilled. Even with the problem gone, it takes a lot of your energy and makes you weaker by not giving you much emotional chargeback. There are, of course, overlaps. However, this is a rough idea. Negative stress often lingers in your mind even after the issue is resolved, leaving traces of anxiety or tension that can affect your overall well-being. Unlike positive stress, it rarely inspires growth or pushes you toward achieving something meaningful, instead creating a cycle of exhaustion.

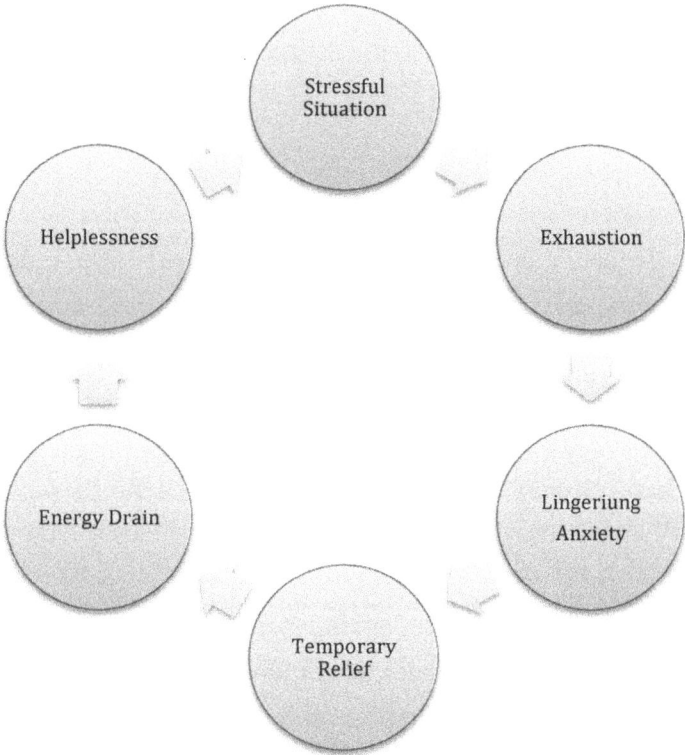

Fig. 3. The Cycle of Exhaustion

It is well-known that negative stress has a damaging effect on your general well-being. It also increases compulsive behaviors, including consumption. When your life is full of negative stress that does not reward you in the end, you may feel a need to distract yourself from it and reward yourself for all that effort and suffering you went through. When it comes to distraction, you are very likely to go for instant gratification because they would require less stress and effort – and you have already exceeded your normal amount of those – and because these are faster. Your mind and body need something immediately in order to recover. Or, this is what it seems.

If you try to go for positive stress instead, it could be very helpful. I know it is easier said than done, but our perception of things is largely in our own hands. We can look at something as a stressful event that scares us or as an interesting challenge. Among my loved ones are people who can handle so much stress without letting it affect them. It almost seems like they enjoy the challenge and get satisfaction from solving these difficult tasks. At the same time, I would be losing my mind from stress and would feel exhausted, anxious, frustrated, or helpless. As I said, I am a work in progress. I've started to realize that everyone's ability to cope with stress is different, often shaped by their experiences, mindset, and habits. Learning from their approach, I've begun exploring ways to strengthen my own resilience, even if it's just one small step at a time.

## Live in the Present – And Appreciate It

As I am writing these lines, I remember how, at a college I worked at, I was consoling a home-sick student. The poor guy was very sad and kept dreaming of going back home to his family but had to stay overseas alone and struggle in this challenging pace of a big foreign city. I told him a bit about my experience in China when I was his age and how I lived there by myself for a year, when my Mandarin was worse than his English, while the English of the people around me was often worse than my Mandarin. I had to practice my body language skills and bury my sense of shame in order to practice and practice until I could evolve into a human being who could explain herself properly. I told him about the dangers and difficulties I had been through when my friend and I traveled alone through the country with no guides or local friends around when our motel room just happened to have no door at all, and when I had to escape from a crazy guy who went after me, and what saved me was the fact that his size was too big for him to chase me through the narrow paths in the crowd without bumping into everyone and everything on his way. And how I also felt home-sick and was trying to draw my brother when sitting in class. And how my lovely Japanese roommate and I cried in the room together because we were homesick. I explained how those experiences, though terrifying and challenging, taught me to trust my instincts and appreciate the kindness of strangers who helped along the way. They also made me value the emotional bonds that gave me strength when I felt the most vulnerable.

And then, I told him about those fun and funny moments I had, people I met, and priceless memories that I treasure and keep in my heart forever. This Japanese roommate has been like my sister ever since, and when we cried like two little girls, my Ukrainian guy friend showed up and spent a good fifteen minutes cheering us up by making fun of himself. These people who could not communicate in English and who we had to interact with through our struggling Mandarin and body language became my very close friends for life and inspired me to learn their languages – this is how I started learning Japanese and Korean. There were so many great moments that I will cherish forever! As for the difficulties, they made me a stronger and smarter person and inspired me to get into better shape and learn to run faster – I had hated running long distances before. People in China were mostly friendly, interesting, and warm-hearted, and I enjoyed communicating with them, learning about their culture, and seeing their day-to-day life. They were filling my every day with something special. Those Chinese teachers loved their students as if we were their younger family members. That taxi driver who became a Formula 1 superstar for me for an hour and, by some magic powers, brought me to my train during rush hour one minute before its departure when, logically speaking, it was impossible. Those ladies at a local supermarket would always have an extra treat to give to us home-sick international students. Those older men selling things on the streets who had a broad smile on their faces and spoke Russian, calling me tovarisch (comrade) and getting upset at me when they learned in conversations that I was no fan of Lenin, Stalin, or Putin. One guy at the market even went as far as saying that I was not a real

Russian and taking away from me a small chair that he had brought me a moment ago. These memories bring a smile to my face to this day. It's funny how even the smallest encounters can leave such lasting impressions, shaping the way I see people and the world. They remind me that human connection, in all its forms—kindness, humor, or even disagreement—can transform fleeting moments into cherished stories.

I told my student that at each point of time we are living a certain experience that will not repeat itself at any other moment. Listen, I said, you will be with your family in two years. You will not be in this class anymore, with these three guys whose contagious laughter I can hear from my work desk, with these other caring classmates of yours who have been trying to make your life better this whole morning with good words and sweet treats, and with your wonderful teachers Sam and Abu — all of who care about you. You will miss them. And you will regret that you did not appreciate your time together. And you may be back home sad about it like you are now about missing home. They are here now, in front of you. So, appreciate and enjoy what you have in front of you now, and then, when the situation changes, you will appreciate and enjoy other moments and things. You can write a letter or an email to your family every day or week describing everything that has been happening to you here and all the things – good or bad, fun or challenging – that you see and experience. Thus, you will let them live these moments with you and make all of your lives richer for it. Taking time to focus on the present will make your days feel more meaningful and help you cherish the connections and experiences you have now. And when you look back someday, you will realize that those little moments you embraced were the ones that truly defined this chapter of your life.

I said to him that when he becomes a Grandpa, what will matter will not be a big number of comfortable days behind, one similar to another, but his experiences and memories—diverse, interesting, challenging, emotional, or at times crazy. These memories will be invisible luggage that will stay in his heart and mind forever and will be something to tell his grandkids over tea.

On a student orientation later on, I told newbies that while they should, of course, be studying and working hard, they should not forget to live and enjoy their youth, as, while their financial success mattered, their treasures in old age would be their memories, adventures, and feelings.

We often focus on what we do not have that we wish we had at the moment. We live in the past by missing something that we used to have before or in the future by waiting to get or experience something that is not here yet. In doing so, we overlook the beauty and opportunities in the present, where life is unfolding right in front of us. Thus, we do not enjoy life in the present and feel miserable and dissatisfied. But, when we look back after a month, a year, or a number of years, we are mad at ourselves for having wasted that time. And then, again, we focus on self-blame and regret, on that past that we missed by regretting that we had missed some other more remote past before. It is like a domino effect. And it is like we are always behind in life, stuck in ruminations over our previous experiences instead of living the current ones. It does not have to be this way. Be where you are, make the best out of it, appreciate and enjoy what you can, and move on to the next stage. Every moment spent dwelling on what could have been is a moment taken away from the potential of the present. By accepting where we are now, with all its imperfections and possibilities, we create space for growth and joy without the burden of what is lost. When we let go of this cycle, we open ourselves up to new opportunities and a deeper sense of fulfillment.

## Go for Positive Motivation and Avoid Labels

Sometimes, persuading yourself does not work, while a harsh word of reality or a threat does magic. Yes, sometimes negative motivation seems more efficient. However, its main weakness is that it often gives short-term results. Negative motivation taps into our fight-or-flight response, triggering an immediate sense of urgency or fear that pushes us into action. While effective at the moment, this kind of motivation can lead to burnout or resentment over time if relied upon too much. The long-term effectiveness of motivation is rooted in positive reinforcement and intrinsic goals, which foster sustainable growth and fulfillment rather than simply reacting to threats or negative pressure.

Negative motivation is there for our survival. It prevents us from acting in a way that may be dangerous for us and protects us from danger. This is a one-time thing or a repetitive sequence of one-time things. It sends us into fight-or-flight mode, which helps us resolve the threatening situation fast and efficiently. But it is not normal for our body to function in this mode for a long period, and if it has to, it can lead to a number of health and emotional issues.

Positive motivation is good for long-term changes and progress. Positive motivation allows you to combine fight-or-flight mode with resting mode. As this is more natural for the body, the body will not fight this as a part of self-defense, which means that your behavior will be more consistent and lasting. It aligns your actions with your intrinsic goals, creating a sense of purpose and fulfillment. Additionally, positive motivation builds resilience by turning setbacks into learning opportunities rather than sources of stress. It also fosters a growth mindset, where progress is celebrated, ensuring sustained motivation over time.

Don't be too harsh on yourself, and don't blame yourself too much for mistakes you make. Understand that these are part of learning and improvement. The fact that you have made these mistakes only means that there is something to work on. Put in the effort, track your progress, and focus on it. Remember, growth often comes from failure, not perfection. Every mistake is an opportunity to refine your approach and move closer to your goal. Be patient with yourself; progress takes time, and consistency is key. Celebrate small wins along the way, as they are stepping stones to greater success.

If you bought yourself a fifth t-shirt of the same type, knowing you do not need it but are still unable to resist it, well, ok, if you do not want to return it, then keep it, use it, and be glad you have it. Be at peace with the things you do. Guilt makes you uncomfortable and thus pushes you to seek more rewards, and material ones are often the fastest and easiest to obtain. Healthy responsibility and a positive mindset activate in you action-based and progress-based emotional rewards and help you improve and reach your goals. Focusing on growth-oriented rewards encourages a deeper sense of fulfillment, which is more sustainable than temporary material gratification.

Think of a better image of yourself, a better you. And then be closer to that person, step-by-step, action-by-action, change-by-change. Imagine you are already that person and do what they would do. Do not label yourself with negative labels. Labels stop and slow us down, and this is simply because everything you do will have to go through the screen of that label, and it will be difficult for you to have faith in yourself when something you do goes against that label. So, accept your mistakes and deal with them; be responsible for them, own them, and love, respect, and believe in yourself regardless. Also, labels are static while we are dynamic, or at least should be such. Labels may slow you down in your growth and stagnate your development. Instead of seeing mistakes as failures, view them as opportunities to evolve. Focus on the present moment, where true growth happens, rather than being stuck in past labels. Believe in your ability to change and improve, and remember that each small step counts toward the person you want to become.

## Don't Rely on a Palm Tree

On a dark summer night, I pushed my indoor palm tree in a tall, heavy pot against the door. It was heavy enough to make opening the door from outside very challenging, at least for a woman. I also put a book on the pot to prop up the door handle so it could not move. But how could I sleep that night if I had to be alert? Following my brother's advice, I took a plastic cup, filled it with metal spoons and forks, and placed it on the edge of the pot. If the pot was to move, the cup would fall and make enough noise to wake me up. That night, I needed to rely on that palm tree for my safety. Though the setup gave me some peace of mind, I couldn't help but feel a nagging sense of vulnerability, unsure if it would truly protect me if something went wrong.

A week before this, an old friend of mine – let's call her T – reached out to me after not being in touch for a couple of years. She said something happened at her old place and she had nowhere to go. T asked if she could stay with me for a few days until she finds a new place. I asked my landlords, and they agreed to give us a week. I communicated this to T, and she moved in to stay with me for the week.

Right away, I started looking for options that she could rent. But T did not seem concerned and did not do any search or contact any of the places I found. I ignored this red flag and explained this to myself by her distress and the idea that she may need a couple of days. Then, I made my main mistake, which was giving her an extra key so she would not be locked out while I was at work, as she would head to the library early in the morning and would come back before me.

T acted strange; she rearranged some items at my home, questioned what I had in the fridge and how I organized it and started mixing her clothes with mine in the closet and laundry basket. Every time I reminded T that she had to move out and asked her if she had found a place, she would say she had a headache or that I was not to worry about it. At that point, I was definitely worried. It felt as though she was settling in permanently, and the discomfort of the situation was beginning to set in.

The evening before the day she needed to move out, T refused to give me back the key or talk to me about her plans. She helped herself to bed and fell asleep or pretended not to hear or see me.

On the day of the story, I had to wake up very early so that she would not escape for the day with the key. When she came out of the shower, I was sitting at the table waiting for her, like special agents waiting for their targets in their houses. She was as silent and non-responsive as a fish. As she silently got ready and rushed to the door, I ran there and blocked the door with my body, demanding she give me back the key. T stared at me silently and tried to push me away from the door. I stood strong. We spent two hours like this by that door. I reminded T about my landlords, laws, and many other things. Nothing seemed to concern her. She stared at me with a strange, cold look and a weird, chilling smile. At some point, she said, "Don't worry, I have a plan for us, and you may like it; it's not too bad." What the heck was that? Good luck not worrying after such a weird phrase. When I calmly asked what she was talking about, she just smiled with a strange smile and kept staring at me.

By that time, I had already texted my boss, saying that I was afraid I could not make it to work due to an emergency. I would not leave T alone in the basement, and I would not let her stay longer. At this point, she was freaking me out. So, this is when I said, fine, you go do what you want, and went to sit at my desk. My plan now was that once she left, I would explain everything to my landlords and ask to change the lock. But she stayed, too. I started to feel trapped in my own home, unable to escape the tension and discomfort of the situation. My initial concern for her well-being had shifted into a fear of what she might do next, and I realized I had to act quickly and wisely before things escalated further.

So, I was sitting at my desk facing the wall and trying to work on something on my laptop and to behave as calmly and naturally as possible. Behind me, staring at me with a deadly and crazy stare, was a girl I had considered a friend just a week ago. She was sitting at my little dining table and drilling my back with her stare as if looking through me, not at me. The silence felt heavy, and the only thing that could be heard was her fingers drumming on the table. I tried to act relaxed but wished she would leave. I also wished some wizard would come to help me extract my key from her. The tension in the air was unbearable, and with every passing minute, I could feel my anxiety growing. The more I tried to focus on my work, the more her presence seemed to dominate the space. It felt as though she was waiting for something, and I couldn't shake the feeling that I was in danger.

"So, Genya," T suddenly said, making me turn around to face her, "Tell me about yourself." What? What kind of request is that? It was so out of place. At this point, I suspected T could be on some drugs or something of the sort. It only got better. Shortly, T started singing a song while staring at me, and the song went something like, "we are going for eternity together." I certainly did not like that idea. Then T ripped my bracelet off my hand and started hysterically laughing while picking up scattered beads from the floor and putting them in her pocket. She also made sure to wish me everything worst under the sky since I was a terrible person, according to her. When reminded that the police may be called if she refuses to leave, she said she would fight them. It took me hours and some sudden public speech talent to get her to leave before the night fell. While my landlords did tell me she could stay one last night, no way I wanted this crazy person there for the night. I had a very uneasy, dark feeling about it. So, she did eventually leave, out of nowhere, giving me a hug and saying, "Love you", which was overturned half an hour later by her WhatsApp message where she was saying how much she hated me and hoped to never see me again, or I would regret it. What a day. Don't forget she still had the key. The one I should have never had or given to her. And now, between me and her possible return was only that palm tree, a book, and a cup of metal cutlery. That was the only safety pillow I had.

One of T's kind wishes was for me to get kicked out of that basement and become homeless. While this did not happen, I must say I felt there was indeed a risk, as my landlords were not very happy about the situation, and rightfully so. Not only have I failed to see T's nature, but I also gave her that key. I was very sorry. We changed the lock the next day, and I did not have any friends over since then. My landlords have always been very sweet people, and I wanted to make sure I do not cause any more inconvenience ever. Looking back, I realized that my inability to set clear boundaries allowed this situation to escalate, and I vowed to be more cautious in the future. Trusting the wrong people, especially when they don't show the same level of respect and care, can lead to uncomfortable and even dangerous situations.

Had I been kicked out or had some of my or my landlords' property been damaged by that lunatic, I would be, how should I put it politely, cooked. And no shoes or shirts that I had would matter. I would have a bunch of things I barely even used instead of savings or some kind of small assets, a real safety pillow. Sometimes, things happen, and when all the hell breaks loose, you want to rely on something more than a palm tree. Events like this and ones that are way worse help put things in perspective and realize what you really need and what you don't. This experience made me realize that material possessions, no matter how important they may seem in the moment, cannot replace the value of stability and security. When you're facing real adversity, it's the intangible things—like your safety, your peace of mind, and your ability to bounce back—that becomes most important. And for these, you need a safety pillow that is only possible when you prioritize and spend wisely instead of surrounding yourself with things you don't really need.

# Chapter 4. Make Neuroscience Your Friend

*"He will win who knows when to fight and when not to fight."*

*– The Art of War, by Sun Tzu.*

We have so far been focusing on the conscious aspect of our behaviours. But there is something big underneath, something that we do not want to fight, as we would not win – our biology, nature, basic neurological structure. Trying to overwrite these with logic and strength would be like trying to swim against a very mighty current; not only will we not progress in the direction we want to go, but we would likely be thrown back. Instead of wrestling with our neurological structure, we may want to understand it and use it to our advantage. Our brain is wired for survival and efficiency, which is why we often rely on automatic responses to perceived threats or discomforts. Understanding these innate impulses can help us better navigate situations and guide our behavior in a way that aligns with our goals rather than fighting against the flow. By understanding how habits are formed and learning how to work with our instincts, we can make lasting changes without constantly battling our biology. This approach not only helps us manage challenges but also makes us feel more in control of our lives.

As I am as much of a neuroscientist as I am a ballerina, I suggest you look deeper into the topic and refer to experts. Here, I will share my surface understanding of it and how it relates to our topic. Neuroscientists may correct me on certain things, but I believe that my description provides a general idea that is enough to benefit our purpose here. My humble goal is to present you with some basics and inspire your further research and thinking on the topic if you find it of interest and use.

## Meet Your Brain

We have all heard how heart and mind can be in opposition to each other, how our brain would tell us one thing but the heart something else. When we say 'heart,' we usually refer to the emotional component that also technically comes from the brain.

Our brain is not on the same page with itself on much deeper levels. It is not only about the emotional vs the logical. Different parts of the brain can literally do their own thing and confuse the hell out of their human. This dissonance is driven by the fact that our brain consists of different regions, each with its specialized role, such as the limbic system for emotions and the prefrontal cortex for logical decision-making. These areas sometimes send conflicting signals, creating confusion and internal conflict. Additionally, our brain's automatic, survival-driven responses can override our rational thinking, especially in stressful or uncertain situations. By understanding that these competing impulses come from different brain areas, we can better navigate our emotions and logic, allowing us to make more balanced decisions despite the internal noise.

To simplify it, there is a prefrontal cortex, the part of the brain that constitutes over ten per cent of the brain's volume and has a lot of functions, including cognitive and executive. It processes the input from the environment, compares it to past experiences, and reacts to these. It controls reflexive behaviors and is involved in planning, self-control, decision-making, and problem-solving while prioritizing long-term goals instead of short-term pleasantries. If you look at the parts of the brain as a friend group, this is your intelligent and logical friend who stays away from trouble, plans long-term, and tries to do the right thing. However, even this logical friend can sometimes be overridden by the emotional and impulsive friend, leading to conflicting decisions and behaviors.

Then, we have the amygdala, the part of the brain most closely associated with fear and emotions. It is this lady who tells your body to panic when a danger is perceived. Have you ever chickened out while watching a scary movie? You know it is just a movie, and the ghost is there on the screen, while you are here on the couch. You even know that the ghost is not even real and people on the screen are actors. And yet, you get all tense and scared. Well, I am definitely a big chicken when it comes to watching horror movies. Heck, even parodies of horror movies get me. Thanks, the amygdala. This little almond-shaped part of the brain cannot tell whether the danger is real or perceived. It has to act quickly. Otherwise, we would not have survived as a species while analyzing the danger. So, the amygdala gives us a signal for a fight-or-flight, and we do what we need to do with this. In my case, I close my eyes, turn my head away from the screen, or cover my face with my jacket. Childish, I know. As a major center for emotion processing, the amygdala also connects memories and your senses, contributing to motivation and learning. This learning is, however, the one that mostly has to do with survival and well-being, as you need to learn and remember behaviors that would benefit you and recognize and remember potentially dangerous ones. Such ones got you in trouble before. In a way, it's like your brain's version of a "survival playlist"—a collection of hits that keep you safe and remind you to stay away from danger, even if they sometimes play on repeat a little too loudly. So, the amygdala would be your emotionally impulsive friend and the one who either throws punches when feeling threatened or gets scared easily and wants to run away upon any sign of potential danger.

The amygdala is not the only emotional friend in the group. It is part of the limbic system responsible for our behavioural and emotional responses. It focuses on behaviors that have to do with our survival, including the fight for light responses. Some other parts of the system that I believe are most relevant here include the hippocampus that is the memory center that forms our episodic memories and produces neurons, and basal ganglia that has to do with reward processing and habit formation, as well as learning that results from these. Think of the hippocampus as your brain's librarian, storing all the life events you've lived through, while the basal ganglia is like your reward-hungry pet, always eager to learn new tricks and get that treat at the end. The limbic region and brain stem are also often referred to as the reptilian brain or lizard brain because of their primal nature and functions. As for the prefrontal cortex, it is, to a large extent, what makes us human and unique as it operates on a more intellectually complex level.

So, now imagine this friend group going out and about and involving in all kinds of experiences and interactions with the outside world. The limbic system is the loudest and quickest to react, while the prefrontal cortex looks at this sub-group and knows that many of their behaviors are stupid. It feels second-hand shame for their mess-ups, as well as guilt and failure for not being able to prevent them from doing stupid things. The amygdala and limbic system often run the show, while the prefrontal cortex watches it helplessly, and all it can do is facepalm.

Now, who would you address if you wanted to change this group's responses? You can talk to the prefrontal cortex all you want. 'I know, right?' The prefrontal cortex will say, shake its head, and keep facepalming. Yet, this is what we do most of the time. We try to plead with the logical part of us, the part that is focused on what is right, reasonable, efficient, and beneficial in the long run. You need to address your limbic system, and it does not talk in complex logical terms. It's like trying to convince your dog to stop eating the couch cushions by reasoning with it – you're going to get a lot of tail wagging and nothing else. This does not bring us far. If we instead get the attention of the emotional sub-group and also make friends with our limbic system by understanding what it wants and how we can strike a deal with it, we will go further, and it will be easier.

As Sun Tzu said, "In battle, there are not more than two methods of attack – the direct and the indirect; yet, these two in combination give rise to an endless series of maneuvers.' There is a lot of flexibility in how we can tackle issues. We do not have to try to suppress any part of our brain; instead, we can act indirectly, understand the basics of its nature, and give it something that it wants to get the result we want. By addressing the root of our impulses and desires, we can guide them with intention and wisdom rather than forcefully trying to eliminate them. This approach requires patience and understanding, but it is through this deeper understanding of our brain's mechanisms that we can foster long-term growth and alignment with our true goals.

## The Dance of the Executive and Limbic Systems

If we generalize and divide our brain into an executive and a limbic system, these two have to get along well in order for us to function successfully. If you picture a dance of two, there needs to be just the right amount of push or pull on both sides. Otherwise, the balance will be lost. Both partners are crucial for the dance. The limbic system is responsible for the rapid processing of immediate dangers or rewards. This happens subconsciously without you thinking about it or assigning it any kind of logical or ethical value. The focus of your limbic system is your survival, for which it sends you signals in the form of cravings or emotions such as pleasure, pain, or fear and does so very quickly before the executive system even gets a chance to step in. This means that, in moments of stress or temptation, the limbic system can override your conscious thoughts, pushing you to react instinctively and without the filter of logic or long-term planning.

The executive system of your brain is the one that processes information and emotions consciously and deliberately, with different factors in mind. It formulates long-term goals and decides the steps to achieve them. There is no instant gratification here; instead, the executive system plans for future rewards to satisfy the cravings and wants of the limbic system.

The potential for a problem lies in the impatience of the limbic system. When it craves something intensely, this is immediate and often overrides all the efforts by the executive system. This is why your will strength by itself may not be enough to keep you from impulsive behaviors. Your conscious will belongs to the executive system that does not even get a chance at action or thought until after the limbic system bombards you with very strong emotions and cravings. In this dance, the limbic system pulls too suddenly and too strongly leaving the executive system little chance of maintaining the balance. This dynamic creates a constant tug-of-war, where the limbic system's desire for immediate satisfaction can derail long-term goals, no matter how much you consciously want to stay on track. To effectively manage this requires not just willpower but strategies that acknowledge and work with the speed and force of the limbic system, allowing the executive system to step in before the craving takes over.

What should we do with this information? I do not have a great answer. I guess that instead of trying to pull back at all times and using up all its energy, the executive system (our conscious brain) can significantly reduce the limbic system's urge to pull strongly by providing frequent rewards to it. Unlike those disarming cravings where you cannot decide what the object of craving is, with these rewards that you volunteer, you can choose better reward options. And hey, who doesn't like a good, well-deserved reward now and then? It's like giving your brain a treat, but with a much healthier and more long-term impact.

## Trick Your Lizard Brain

So, does this mean that you can trick your lizard brain? Which, technically, means that one part of your brain can trick the other. Yes, this seems to be the case. More complex systems within your brain can trick the more primal and reflexive ones. Let me start guessing and speculating. Please feel free to criticize and correct me here. My lizard brain will not feel threatened by that, I promise.

If you can get yourself scared by tricking the amygdala into thinking that you are in danger when watching a horror movie, can you do the opposite? I cannot claim for sure what it was, but I remember that when I was little when I craved ice cream but could not have it, I would often imagine eating it, and, interestingly enough, I would feel as if I actually did. I remember the taste and texture, the sensation of eating it, and shortly after, it felt like I just ate my favorite ice cream. It's like your mind was giving you a mini-ice cream party, no calories, just pure joy! But on a deeper note, this shows how powerful our mind can be in influencing our experience of reality. In his famous book Phsycho-Cybernetics, Maxwell Maltz claims that our brain does not differentiate between our real experiences and vividly imagined ones. This means that visualization and mental imagery can trigger the same brain reactions as actual events or performances. This concept, suggested by Maltz, paved the way for numerous theories on visualization principles as it comes to one's success, capabilities, and opportunities, and this phenomenon underlines how our thoughts and emotions can shape our perception of satisfaction or deprivation.

What if you imagine actually getting an item you want, but instead of that illusionary thinking where you picture a better, non-yet-existent version of yourself magically flowing through not-yet-existent, successful, and happy life of yours, you imagine your actual day with it, very realistically, the way you currently are? You diligently think of how you would get it, bring it home, and use it in your everyday life without any beautification of your self-image or the image of your current life.

First, you may see that this item would not magically transform your life. Secondly, you may be able to trick your lizard brain and not want it as much after that. Why so? This is because the anticipation of getting the item will be gone. See, the thing is that our limbic system is big on anticipation - of either danger or reward. This makes sense, as our lizard brain would need to be guessing where danger or reward could be coming from and connecting these to strongly negative or positive emotions and memories. When the anticipation is gone because something already happened (even if in your imagination only), the lizard brain does not hold on to that item as much anymore since now it makes its way to other parts of the brain team. It's almost like when you finally eat that piece of chocolate you've been craving, and the intense longing vanishes, leaving you just enjoying the moment without the obsessive fixation. On a deeper level, this shift is your brain prioritizing what's real, moving the focus from immediate gratification to broader, longer-term goals. By using your imagination to let the event unfold in your mind, you're reducing the emotional grip of that desire, allowing other parts of your brain to take over and make more rational decisions.

Another way to trigger your lizard brain could potentially be connecting undesirable behavior to negative emotions and memories. Great, you say, why then does it not work to be upset over spending too much on those shoes? This was something pretty negative. This must be because this experience, although negative, was not closely linked to your survival and was, therefore, none of your lizard brain's business. I mean, let the front of the brain deal with all this smart stuff; the lizard is not interested in it as long as it does not directly threaten you at the moment. Essentially, your lizard brain is focused on immediate survival and threats, not on managing your finances or keeping your impulses in check. Now, if you were to receive an epic physical response after you bought unneeded items, like if the shoes jumped out of the box and started biting you, the lizard would make it its task and responsibility to try to stop you next time. You would be sent into a fight or flight mode, which, most likely, would show itself as you ran away from the store screaming bloody murder or destroying those predatory shoes.

Seriously, though, I think we all have, at some point, had food poisoning. Remember? I bet you do. And I bet all your body does. We all know the feeling when you just can't look at food the same way after one bad experience—it's like your brain hits the panic button on repeat every time you see it again. I haven't eaten ground beef for years since I once had food poisoning after a bad experience with it. My inner lizard instantly brings up those not-so-fun memories and causes in me such a strong flight response that I instantly evaporate from any vicinity of the dish. You could say I have beef with beef. By no means do I suggest that you put yourself in any danger or harmful ways for the sake of tricking the lizard. This is why I believe in influence through reward rather than punishment.

## Start the Perpetual Motion Dopamine Machine

There is no limit to perfection. Therefore, there is no limit to self-improvement and progress. Suppose you start deriving rewards from the progress, from the completion of certain steps, from the anticipation of these little milestones and improvements. In that case, you will have started a perpetual motion machine of dopamine. This can be achieved through a high level of self-discipline. The prefrontal cortex, you say right away. Yes, that's right. You would need to work with your prefrontal cortex while restraining the mischievous easily tempted lizard from any impulsive steps that would compromise the long-term goal. In the meantime, you would need to find ways to make the lizard happy or distract it until the lizard learns to derive rewards from the right things. Gamify your progress, turn tasks into fun challenges, or track wins with a reward system. Celebrate small wins, a happy dance, or a quick treat can train your brain to enjoy the journey.

In addition to making and meeting goals, another great way to maintain a continuous and healthy dopamine supply has to do with human connection and relationships. According to Dr. Robert Waldinger, whom I had the pleasure of listening to on the Diaries of CEO YouTube channel, it is people and memories that turn our purely limbic pleasure into enjoyment. This real enjoyment comes from you doing things with people and remembering them. Enjoyment, according to Dr. Waldinger, consists of two main components, which are happiness and satisfaction – the joy you get after a struggle. Both goal-based and relationship-based types of enjoyment involve delayed gratification. Find joy in shared experiences, spend time with others on activities that foster connection and collaboration, like cooking together, playing a sport, working on a creative project, or helping each other solve problems and do daily tasks. The bonds and memories you build will bring lasting fulfillment. Celebrate your struggles and reframe obstacles as milestones in an exciting journey. Reflect on how overcoming them adds richness to your story and makes the eventual satisfaction even sweeter. In short, if you want to start a perpetual motion dopamine machine, you limit your instant gratification and go for the delayed type. Sorry, lizard brain, let's negotiate.

## Negotiating With Your Lizard Brain

So, you cannot ignore your reptilian brain, and you should not do so either, as - come on - your limbic system goes out of its way for the sake of your survival and safety. You also cannot constantly be tricking it, as, first of all, it's not fair to treat your honest and dedicated friend like this, and, secondly, you still want it to be smart, accurate, and function properly. Therefore, it seems reasonable to me to negotiate with the lizard. Teach it healthy rewards by redirecting its cravings to habits that benefit you, like substituting a snack craving with a quick walk or an energizing playlist. Keep it engaged by giving it short-term wins that align with long-term goals, like tackling a small, satisfying task to stay motivated while on a larger mission.

Give your limbic system its craved rewards, but choose what type of rewards you give to it. For example, when or even before it starts craving unhealthy salty snacks, make a yummy healthy salad with a bit of salty flavor to it; if you crave processed sugars, choose fruits or other healthier desserts. If you wish to binge-watch a series, you may want to do exercises while doing so, and if you are listening to podcasts you got hooked on, you may want to take a long walk while doing so. The key is in either replacing the reward with a better option or accompanying it with such. This way, you encourage your reward system to tune into healthier dopamine sources and move more towards making them your main sources. Layer rewards by pairing your favorite treats or shows with productive habits, like enjoying a special drink while organizing your workspace. Gradually, your brain will associate the positive feelings with productive activity. Introduce time-based challenges by setting mini-goals, such as completing a short task during the span of a podcast episode or doing stretches during ad breaks. This keeps things engaging and fun. Use variety to your advantage by rotating different healthy habits alongside your usual rewards to keep the experience fresh and prevent boredom.

Sometimes, when I crave to excessively play games on my PC or phone, I know that accomplishing certain tasks or projects that I have or learning things activates similar responses in my system, and I go for such activities instead. When I crave to buy a new dress for no real reason, I sometimes set requirements first, such as first, I need to achieve certain fitness goals. Interestingly, in the process of such, I often stop caring about the dress since those cool chemicals keep flowing into my system from the exercise and all the satisfaction that comes with it.

Sometimes it may seem that in this extremely busy time and world, it is difficult to regularly keep your lizard brain happy. What we forget is that, under various circumstances, we can use the senses available to us at the moment. You can't actively do other things as you are focused on a task or routine. Do you have your hands and eyes busy? Listen to things – podcasts, music, audiobooks. Can't do that? Work on your legs by stretching them or doing some light exercises while performing other tasks. Most of the time, there is a sense and a group of muscles available at the moment that you can go to in order to provide yourself with some gratification, ideally a healthy one - be it exercise interesting, educating podcasts, or anything else. You can also get your limbic system distracted from its other cravings by doing so.

## Blessing and Curse of Homeostasis

Have you noticed that no matter how difficult some periods of your life can be, you still get to smile and laugh sooner or later, even when in distress? Likewise, when life is good, you will find yourself in a bad mood sometimes. All organisms use the self-regulating process of homeostasis to maintain stability. This is needed in order to adjust to the surrounding conditions in a way that is best for survival. This is a blessing as it helps all living beings survive. This can also be a curse when it minimizes the positive in our lives, devaluing our dopamine input and, therefore, putting us on a hedonic treadmill. No matter how awesome or terrible something is, our body naturally returns to its original state. We cannot be happy or suffer forever. So, suppose you shower yourself with all types of rewards coming from entertainment, food, consumption, and other types of gratifying behaviors. In that case, homeostasis will bring the intensity of all the dopamine input down so that you do not die of pleasure or something. Seriously, though, huge levels of pleasure on a lasting basis are not natural for an organism and, therefore, are deemed unstable and potentially dangerous. So, each reward will then bring less and less joy until you become a dopamine junkie fighting for the next dose. Each next dose will require more and more gratifying behavior, and you will be stuck on that treadmill.

Is there a way to avoid this hedonic treadmill that homeostasis helps enable? There must be. The joy and fulfillment that one gets from the family, friendship, faith, or service to others cannot depreciate in their dopamine value; it is long-lasting and strong, leading to more joy and fulfillment, as love brings on more love, and the true empowerment comes from doing good deeds for others. Cultivate a sense of purpose by focusing on meaningful actions that contribute to the well-being of others, which creates a deeper, sustainable source of happiness that doesn't rely on external rewards.

Be mindful of the balance by recognizing when you're overloading your reward system and intentionally stepping back to reset it. Mix up your rewards by introducing smaller, more meaningful pleasures rather than relying on big bursts of gratification. This keeps your brain engaged and helps prevent the diminishing returns of overstimulation. Recognize the cycle by acknowledging that life's ups and downs are natural and don't diminish the value of the highs or the lessons from the lows. Practice gratitude regularly to counteract the hedonic treadmill and remind yourself of the unique joy in the everyday moments. Introduce novelty into your routine to disrupt homeostasis and keep your brain engaged with fresh experiences, avoiding the trap of monotony.

## Dopamine Detox

You see how we are dopamine junkies. Well, a lot of us. If you believe you are not, think again. If you still believe that, then I am sending you my respects and admiration. A lot of us, however, at one point or another, even if for short periods, become dopamine junkies. We try to get as much dopamine as possible, where possible, and, thanks in part to homeostasis, we feel less and less gratification from each dose; we get desensitized.

The concept of dopamine detox has become popular in recent years. Like when you cleanse your body by staying away from junk food and such, in case of a dopamine detox, you keep yourself from pleasurable activities for a period to reset your brain's neurochemical system and dopamine receptors and to help you break free from addictive behaviors, if any.

Among pleasurable activities that you may want to stay away from during your dopamine detox are so-called dopamine boosters, such as drinking alcohol, consuming drugs, sugar, and caffeine, overeating, playing video games, and spending time on social media. These dopamine boosters are largely linked to addictions. I would also argue it is good to stay away from consumption of unnecessary items. You can either stay away from these or significantly limit the dopamine boosters. It may not feel good at first, as you may feel bored, restless, or uncomfortable in some way. However, the idea is that you help reset your system and find much more enjoyment in smaller amounts of pleasurable activities without having to constantly fill yourself with dopamine boosters. Redirect your energy into new hobbies or interests that require focus and engagement, like learning a new skill or exploring nature, which naturally offer long-lasting satisfaction. Practice mindfulness and meditation to help you sit with discomfort, easing the transition and training your brain to find peace without relying on external stimuli.

You can find plenty of information regarding dopamine detox online. There are experts on the topic sharing their experiences and tips. I strongly suggest you look into this. For me, this concept has been of much help.

## Dopamine's Least Favourite Cousin

Dopamine has siblings and cousins. Among them are feel-good hormones like endorphin, serotonin, and oxytocin, and those related to stress, like adrenaline, noradrenaline, and, perhaps, the least favorite cousin, cortisol. These two dislike each other to the extent that they prefer not to show up at the same family reunions so they do not run into each other. This is because cortisol is the main hormone responsible for stress. It can control your mood, motivation, and fear. It is produced in the adrenal gland and other tissues and is released in bigger quantities due to stress. While cortisol has many crucial functions in the body, it also can suppress the immune system, damage cells in the hippocampus, resulting in negative effects on learning and long-term memory, and disrupt many other processes in the body, presenting risks in pregnancy and overall, not doing much good to you if you are exposed to it for extended periods.

Dopamine and cortisol do not like each other that much. Cortisol is the second option for the family if dopamine does not show up at the party. When dopamine levels are low, cortisol is the backup energy hormone that allows the body to function in the lack of dopamine. While it is supposed to be a temporary fix until dopamine shows up, cortisol does not improve dopamine levels. It does not want to see more of dopamine, remember? Instead, cortisol invites its sibling adrenaline. These two, while making you feel energetic, are believed to contribute to anxiety, restlessness, difficulty in sleeping, and obesity.

So, we generally want to have our dopamine levels reasonably high and our cortisol levels reasonably low. Now, what if I told you that, among other things, increased cortisol levels in our body are clutter? According to different studies, it puts you in fight or flight mode. Tidying up your physical space can help reduce stress, creating an environment that promotes calm and focus. Organizing your surroundings, even in small steps, can lead to a sense of accomplishment that boosts dopamine while lowering cortisol. Incorporating minimalism into your daily life can further reduce overwhelming stimuli, allowing you to feel more in control and centered, paving the way for greater mental clarity and emotional balance.

Clutter, logically, is very related to consumerism. While it is possible to have clutter while not overconsuming, it is definitely more difficult to stay clutter-free when you have too many things. And this is in addition to you stressing over spending time and money on something you could definitely live without. So, when you buy yourself an item number gazillion-five that you do not really need, remember that after that instant rush of low-intensity dopamine, you are looking at increasing your cortisol in the longer run.

In turn, the less cortisol and the more dopamine you have at any given moment, the less you crave instant gratification. Managing stress through relaxation techniques or exercise helps keep cortisol in check, ensuring the feel-good hormones have room to thrive. Developing healthy coping strategies, such as journaling or deep breathing, can reduce cortisol's impact and encourage a more balanced emotional state.

## Dopamine - Between Reward and Addiction

While dopamine is essential in our reward system, it also plays an important role in addiction; the brain scan of a heroin addict is similar to that of an addicted gamer, and traits of it are present in the brains of shopping addicts. One of the reasons why our brain can get addicted through dopamine is that dopamine production has more to do with anticipation than the reward itself; that 'maybe' effect is exactly what one experiences when gambling, playing video games, scrolling, or checking how many new likes you get on social media or shopping. What makes it so addictive is the unpredictable character of when the reward may come and what exactly it will be. When you shop for a specific item, it is different. But when you shop for leisure, you do not even know what you are looking for and what you will find and get, at what store and when, which makes the act of going shopping more addictive. The element of surprise keeps the brain hooked, making it crave more. To shop more healthily, it may be a good idea to only go for what you need and when you need it. If you get something extra, then be it, but at least you will have a goal in mind and minimize leisure shopping.

Dopamine reinforces behaviors that previously increased its production in your brain. It creates that memory of a positive experience. When you see a fast-food restaurant, you remember that delicious flavor you tasted last week; you associate a store with a 'high' you got last time after you purchased an item. And this is how a rewarding behavior can become an addictive behavior. What stands in between this and addiction is your choice of where to derive your dopamine from. Once again, if you choose to derive most of your dopamine from healthy sources and activities, you will leave less space for potentially addictive things. By consciously choosing to engage in activities that nurture personal growth, like learning or exercise, you create a healthier feedback loop that doesn't rely on instant gratification. Incorporating mindfulness can help you break the automatic associations and give you more control over where you seek pleasure, allowing you to redirect your focus away from potentially harmful dopamine-driven habits.

# Chapter 5. You Are Being Tricked Into Consumption

## Credit Card Trap

*"We spend the money that we don't possess"*

*Ka-Ching! is a song written by Robert Lange and Shania Twain and recorded by Shania Twain.*

As a teenager, I remember the song; it was released in 2003 and was shown on musical channels on TV in Europe, as well as played on radio. It focused on consumerism in a "greedy little world" where every child was taught "to earn as much as they can, then turn around and spend it foolishly." The video opened with the sounds of a cash register ringing and ended with a poisonous snake that the woman saw on the floor. Pretty deep. If you have not heard this song, I do suggest it, as every line in it is meaningful.

When I was little, we used to read fairy tales where there would be a magic stick – all you needed to do was point at something and make a wish - and voila, witness it done. Our constant, although often subconscious, desire to look for shortcuts and easy solutions is somewhat the wish of a child. Their fairy tale characters had a magic stick. Only this 'wish' system has gone through the adult world and realism and has become more covert. In the lives of many of us, there is a magic stick for adults – a credit card. Just like a magic stick in a fairy tale, the credit card offers an illusion of free and easy instant gratification, enabling us to get what we want immediately without considering the long-term consequences. However, just as in fairy tales, the temporary magic of the credit card can come with a price, leading to consequences like debt or financial stress when we forget to stay grounded in the realities of responsible spending.

No matter how much money you really have, how big or small your income is, and how much you spend—as long as it is within your credit limit — another item is yours. You do not feel like you are spending money the same way you do when you hold cash. Credit cards create an illusion that you have money when all you have is debt. This psychological trick makes it easier to justify impulse purchases, as the immediate consequences are not felt, and the bill is delayed. The detachment between the action of spending and the reality of paying later makes it harder to track how much you're actually spending over time. Moreover, the ease of swiping a card without the physical sensation of handing over cash can lead to overspending and a lack of awareness, which can result in more debt and financial stress in the long run. And what happens with a debt is that you will have to pay it off later. The magic spell will wear off once the limit is reached. If you do not reach the limit, the magic will continue, and you will keep getting access to resources you have not earned yet. This means that you are borrowing money from your future because you will have to earn this money later to pay your debt. So, by spending the money you do not own at the moment, you automatically decide that your future needs are not as important as your current ones and are OK to be affected by your present purchases. This mindset can create a cycle where short-term gratification consistently outweighs long-term financial stability, leading to feelings of stress or regret once the bills arrive. Additionally, by prioritizing immediate desires over future needs, you risk compromising your ability to plan for essential life events, such as emergencies, retirement, or other future goals. Now, think about it this way – do you want your future self – in a week, month, or a year – to save on everything you possibly can work even harder than you do now, and enjoy even less financial freedom? Another fancy party, new bag, or a new iPhone – with a perfectly well-functioning previous model in your possession – means that when the dopamine leaves your system soon after the purchase, you will be left without this amount that you could have spent on something else or even simply required for your basic needs. You could have made yourself or someone you care about much happier on a quality level had you used it differently.

### Tips and Exercises:

1) While you keep paying many bills with your credit card – it is more convenient – you may want to consider putting aside a certain amount of money in cash for other expenses. If you would like to go further with this, you can split these into several stacks for different purposes—groceries, social events, meals, clothing, etc. Or, as you may still need to use a credit card to order things online, for example, you can instead decide on amounts for each category based on how much you actually have in you're a account (debit). This approach helps create a clear budget, making it easier to stay on track and avoid overspending, ensuring that you're only spending what you truly have available.

2) Sometimes, keeping your money in cash may not be the best idea, as you may get a little interest if you keep it in your savings account or because you have loans and debts you would like to pay before a penalty comes your way. In this case, consider using a budgeting app – there are many of those for smartphones – that will help you track all of your expenses and the budget remaining for each category. When you make any payment, quickly enter the date, payment amount, and description under the right category in the app– it will take you a moment. This method also allows you to see trends in your spending habits, helping you make better financial decisions and identify areas where you could save. See how much is left, before what you earned this month is exceeded by what you spent, or how much savings you have, and what categories you go over budget on. Alternatively, you can download a spreadsheet of your transactions and mark categories.

3) Another solution you may want to consider is limiting your budget for each shopping trip you make – and the easiest way to do this is to only take the amount you allow yourself. Let's say you withdraw a hundred dollars and go to a supermarket or a mall. You need to buy things, making sure that you stick to your budget, and you simply do not have a choice because all you've got is that one one-hundred-dollar bill. Let's say there is an emergency or an unforeseen circumstance. Then you can go look for your credit

card, but this extra amount will get deducted from your next shopping budget. This method also helps you practice discipline in your purchases, making sure you don't impulse-buy things you don't truly need. By physically limiting your cash on hand, you also avoid the temptation of overspending with a credit card, which may lead to accumulating unnecessary debt.

Now, this being said, of course, sometimes we all do need to go over the budget. But this is what credit cards and credit lines are for. These are helpful; we just need to use them wisely. One key to using credit cards responsibly is to always pay off your balance in full each month to avoid high-interest charges and accumulating debt. Another important point is to only use credit for necessary purchases or emergencies, not for impulse buys or things you cannot afford at the moment. Lastly, it's essential to track your credit usage regularly to ensure you stay within manageable limits and don't rely too heavily on credit, maintaining a healthy balance between your needs and future obligations.

## Illusion of Urgency

I was sitting in the lobby of a dentist's office, feeling awkward and laughing at myself. What on earth made me buy this dumbbell now in this specific London Drugs store when I could buy it at a different time in a store much closer to my home? Now I was sitting in the lobby holding that big round dumbbell like an idiot and responding with a smile to the looks I was receiving. Not only was I now entering the dentist's office like this, but I was to later enjoy all the beauty of commuting on a train during the rush hour, moving that ten-pound dumbbell from one hand to the other while also trying to hold on to the rails. Amazing.

All this was because I had arrived early and decided to go to the store nearby and get myself an ice cream. Of course, not only did I get an ice cream, but also a bunch of other things and that dumbbell. When I saw it, I immediately thought of how good it would be for me to exercise daily, and without giving it another thought, I grabbed it and proceeded to checkout.

A lot of our buying decisions are made impulsively on the spot. If we stopped for a moment and thought about it, we would realize that if we do need the item, which is often not the case, we could still buy it at a more convenient time or location.

Now, how about sales and limited-time offers? Well, many stores mark their items as being 'on sale' when, in fact, they are not. They pretend that items normally cost more, but if you check, the 'temporary' sale that you should make sure not to miss out on is not temporary at all. It is like with those follow-up sales emails from people trying to sell you services or products where they claim in their titles that something is the last chance, and then, in a month, in two, and three, you still get similar emails with the 'last chance' on. The sense of urgency, related to the fear of missing out, often pushes consumers towards impulsive purchases. Recognizing these marketing tactics can help you pause and make more thoughtful decisions rather than acting on impulse. And even if this urgency of a unique opportunity was real, do you think that maybe you could live with the risk of potentially paying a couple more dollars in the future for some of the items that you later decide to actually buy? Your call. I decided that I could live with that risk.

## Store Strategies

Do you know that stores and malls use a number of strategies and psychological tricks to attract a consumer's attention and make them buy things? Even the colors of the interior and the manner in which items are placed on shelves are not random. For instance, stores often use warm colors like red and yellow to evoke a sense of urgency and excitement, encouraging quicker decision-making. They also strategically place impulse items near checkout counters to entice last-minute purchases, knowing that the closer something is to you, the more likely you are to buy it. You can find a number of videos on YouTube or articles online on this topic. This is a fact. And, if you were a retail business owner, would you not use all possible big and little tricks to make people want to buy more from you?

Let us imagine a story. Robert was tired after a stressful and busy day at work. On top of that, he was hungry, and as a result of all of those mentioned above, he was craving an instant reward in the form of a quick and tasty evening snack. He went into a local supermarket and saw right in front of his eyes items that looked delicious and were pre-cooked. The label stated that it should only take three minutes to prepare and had an image of a happy family on it. Robert was tired, and this was what he needed: something fast and yummy. He put the can in his shopping cart – he was too tired to carry a basket. The supermarket was big and had all types of things, and the cart was big, too, and could fit many of them. Soap? Yes, sure, he will need it soon anyway. The store's lighting was designed to create a relaxed atmosphere, and the aisles were intentionally wide, making him feel like he had plenty of time and space to browse, even though his mind was focused only on satisfying his immediate hunger. There were many kinds, and he took the one that was at the level of his eyes – too tired and lazy to do a good investigation and search. What a nice mug! It had the name of his favorite sports team on it. And it was big. He took it for his office – it would look nice, inspire him, and have a big enough capacity to allow him to not go refill it every half an hour. In a matter of minutes, he filled half of his shopping cart. He was already waiting in line when his bored eyes saw chocolate bars and chewing gum right before the cashier's stand. He automatically took some – it wouldn't hurt to treat himself to some sugar at work during low times, and of course, his breath must be fresh. By the time he checked out, he had collected in his cart many more things than he had planned, and that night, he spent a lot more money than he had expected.

Twenty minutes later, at home, Robert remembered that he had more than enough soap to wash himself and a family of ten for another month. He opened his cupboard to place newly bought cans and discovered that there had already been other similar cans waiting for his attention and not willing to give their place to the newcomers. The next morning, when taking another bag to work, he found a pack of chewing gum that must have been sitting there for a month or so. As he glanced around his home, Robert realized that the act of buying had become a habit, not driven by need but by impulse, leaving him surrounded by items he hadn't fully thought through.

So, what was that? Let's look closer into the situation. Firstly, Robert was tired and was looking for something that would require minimum effort, be fast, and easy. Stores tend to be located at places close to densely populated areas or city centers – basically, crowded places. So, he craved a snack, looked around, and boom, there was a store right around the corner. Secondly, everything in the store looked neat, nice, and relaxing; color combinations were pleasant, and there were many warm colors – like yellow and orange - that inspired hunger. The music was relaxing and refreshing at the same time. All of this made him feel comfortable and want to spend more time there – finally, after all the stress of the day, he was in a comfortable zone. He was looking for easy and fast solutions. All products were organized in a way that it was extremely easy to find anything you wanted, and most promoted – often more expensive – products were placed at eye or chest level so that people would notice them easier. Shopping carts are convenient but dangerous – they make you buy more things because, firstly, they are bigger, and, secondly, you roll them and do not feel the weight of everything you put there. I have many times been surprised at the number of things I bought and how heavy my bags were—after a checkout; all these items traveled from the cart into my hands.

And, surely, the supermarket itself is another trick: you get it all at once, things just throw themselves at you, and you buy what you need and what you do not need. Robert came to buy a snack, a dinner. What did he end up buying? More snacks and junk food, soap, a mug, chocolates, chewing gum, and many other items. If we remember that he went to the supermarket when he was very tired, and that weakened his analytical abilities, it makes sense that he bought a lot of things that he saw on his way through the isles and instantly thought he would need. This is the power of convenience and impulse – the store capitalizes on our fatigue and distracted minds, making us buy without questioning. And this brings us to a phenomenon called an impulse purchase. This is an unplanned purchase of a product or service based on a decision that was made right before the purchase. This is also exactly what happened to Robert when he bought chocolates and chewing gum. And yes, the areas right before the cashier stand are among the favorite spots for brands to place their goods. Can you guess why? Correct, because everyone will see them and because people get bored while waiting in line, which gives them time for impulsive purchases. These are also usually inexpensive little products because impulse purchase behavior normally occurs within lower price ranges; if something is expensive enough to notably affect your budget, you may think twice before you buy it. This strategic placement taps into the "last-minute" mindset, where consumers, already committed to purchasing, are more likely to grab small, affordable items without overthinking them.

## Dark Side of the Bright Light Bulb?

When the light bulb was made brighter, it was a good change. However, some believe that the reason behind it was not to make everyone's lives more comfortable but to decrease the longevity of the light bulb to increase consumption. Others, however, argue that this is a myth as, from the engineering perspective, for a light bulb to last longer, it would be dimmer and less efficient.

If we leave those light bulbs alone and assume there was no ulterior motive there, it is no secret that these days, however, many items tend not to last as much as they used to before; their quality is intentionally made poorer so consumers buy more. Sure enough, if everything we were buying was to last us a lifetime, or at least many years, who would be constantly buying new items to replace the old ones? If, however, items have a shorter life span, much more profit can be made by selling more.

This phenomenon is called planned obsolescence, which, according to the Cambridge Dictionary, is "a situation in which goods are deliberately made or designed so that they do not last for a long period." Planned obsolescence is now extremely widespread in all industries, from clothing to hardware. According to Giles Slade's work, 'Made to Break: Technology and Obsolescence in America,' the phenomenon started in the early twentieth century with household appliance replacement, and noticeable obsolescence was introduced in 1913 and was related to the automotive industry. About a decade later, the phenomenon spread to textile and fashion, watches, radios and many more industries and products.

So, if we do leave light bulbs alone, should we talk about the watch industry instead? In the late 19th century, top watch companies in America produced extremely high-quality, reliable watches that were also low-priced. At the very end of the century, the Yankee watch by Ingersoll was extremely popular as it cost a dollar (an average daily wage at the time) and lasted long. Besides, the watch came with a guarantee of a free replacement should the watch go wrong. To the company's surprise, they hardly ever saw their watches be returned for replacements, as busy working-class owners simply threw out old watches and bought new ones since they were so affordable. According to Giles Slade, it was at around the same time that the phrase so commonly used today, "instant gratification," started being introduced in magazines. The watch owners wanted their new watches instantly and preferred the quick solution over that dollar that they could save by waiting for their replacement.

Without going into more details and history, we can conclude that planned obsolescence has since been increasingly introduced as a practice in many industries. Shoes and clothes are not made to last long, neither do many appliances, pieces of furniture, you name it. Even updates on smartphones were admittedly designed to slow smartphones down to force consumers to buy new phones that otherwise would not be needed. This trend not only drives consumerism but also contributes to environmental degradation, as more goods are disposed of, creating waste that fills landfills. Additionally, it fuels a cycle of dissatisfaction, where consumers are conditioned to believe that they constantly need the latest model, fostering a culture of short-lived satisfaction over long-term value.

## The items we own are not forever - and it's ok.

Now, what do we do with this knowledge? Is there much we can do at all as it relates to our consumption habits? Perhaps not much. However, simply acknowledging this phenomenon makes it easier to plan and have more accurate expectations as it relates to how many items we may require, at what frequency, and how much these can cost us. This can save us some unexpected frustration, as well as a tendency to keep items that can no longer be used although bought not long ago. If we acknowledge the limited life cycle of our items, we may hoard them less and may instead enjoy the item while it lasts and then, when it can no longer be used or fixed, will say goodbye to it and replace it with another item. This awareness could also encourage us to seek out more sustainable options, opting for higher-quality, longer-lasting items that may initially cost more but prove to be more economical and environmentally friendly in the long run.

We need to understand that when we buy something, we do not buy it forever. So, let's say a pair of shoes cost you fifty dollars. You buy it with a subconscious belief that it will now always be yours. What often happens next is that in a year or two, these shoes do not serve their purpose the way they used to – they may get torn, dirty upon any fix, or otherwise affected. You, however, may still keep these since, in your subconscious mind, you bought these to belong to you forever; you did not borrow them.

But did you? Look at it this way – you can stick to the idea of buying an item and therefore maintaining its ownership forever, until it is sitting somewhere in the depth of your closet without being used and only taking up space there. Or, you can look at it as an item you bought for a certain period - for as long as it lasts you. And then you say goodbye to the item and buy another item instead. Just this change of perspective can do wonders. At least, for me, it did.

## Online Shopping – Don't even get me started.

Yeah, don't get me started on this one. And I bet most people can say the same. Once you open an online store and start browsing, you often end up buying more things than you intended to. While at a physical store, there is at least that limit to how much you can carry away with you, the online realm offers you unlimited goods without you having to lift your bottom and put in any amount of physical effort. The convenience of one-click purchases and the endless scrolling through options create a sense of urgency and excitement, making it hard to resist buying things you don't need. Additionally, online shopping often uses algorithms to suggest products based on your browsing history, subtly nudging you toward more purchases that align with your interests, further fueling the desire to buy without second thoughts.

To make things worse, you just punch in your credit card information, and many apps and sites will offer to remember it for future purchases. Ta-dam! That extra step that would allow you an extra minute to think about it while you enter your card details (and often look for your credit card first) is now gone, and the impulsivity gets the best of you as you just swipe right on the screen or click that big bright button. This button itself is another trick, as its visual component and a user-friendly, super easy, and inviting interface make it even easier and more tempting for you to buy things.

But there is also another psychological trick behind online shopping and deals, as these manipulate one's limbic system. According to many interviewed shopaholics, finding new items of interest or new deals often feels to them like gambling. Indeed, like in gambling, one cannot know where and when a reward may come if it does, and what the reward would be. The anticipation of a possible unpredictable reward is associated with dopamine more than the very fact of receiving an award. With the deals that you seem to be getting, you put more and more items into your cart. At the checkout, you see the total costs, taxes, and shipping fees, but hey, you have already come this far, so you might as well proceed with the purchase and finish the whole thing. This "sunk cost fallacy" keeps you locked into the buying cycle, where the more you invest in the process, the harder it is to back out, even if it's financially irrational. Moreover, limited-time offers and countdown timers create a sense of urgency, prompting you to act quickly without thinking through the purchase, further tapping into that fear of missing out on a potential deal.

Let's also not forget that the algorithm analyzes our preferences and tastes, and we are already presented with the choice of items that we are likely to be interested in. All our previous purchases online lead to us being exposed to more similar items. This constant exposure creates a sense of familiarity and comfort, making it easier to click "add to cart" without second-guessing, as the algorithm essentially feeds us what we think we want. Over time, the algorithm can shape our desires and reinforce specific consumer habits, often leading us to buy things we may not have considered if left to our own devices. Additionally, these tailored suggestions often bypass our natural decision-making processes, nudging us toward impulsive purchases by capitalizing on our previous buying patterns and preferences.

So, what do we do? Give yourself time between wanting and buying. Add items to a wish list instead. Believe me, from my wish lists on Amazon, I remember only buying a couple of items, if that; the rest I happily forgot about.

# Chapter 6. More Tips on Building Consumerism Resistance

## Some Math - Magic of Big Numbers

Do you remember that exercise at school where you were to calculate a number of possible combinations that would include a few numbers? Well, I do. If let's say we have three numbers, 1, 2, and 3, we can have 1, 2, 3, 12, 13, 21, 23, 31, 32, 123, 132, 213, 231, 312, and 321. This is fifteen different numbers when you do not use any of the numbers (1, 2, or 3) more than once. Now, if you think that you do not have enough clothing, shoes, or accessories, think of an approximate number you have of each category and make a rough calculation of how many combinations you can get out of these. I am not saying you should now go count all you have and sit with a calculator for another hour – a rough idea is more than enough. See, you can combine each pair of shoes with a large number of items from your wardrobe; you can match your pants, skirts, scarves with a number of shirts, blouses, tops, jackets, etc. You can go by color: white top, black bottom, blue accessories, or black bottom, white top, blue accessories, and so on, like with 123, 213, 321, 132, 231, 312. Now, if you also take into consideration other details, like belts, purses, hairstyles, and makeup, then your number will grow even bigger. You could even challenge yourself to create new combinations you've never tried before—who knows what fresh looks you might discover? And remember, your creativity plays a massive role in how far you can stretch those numbers—fashion is as much about imagination as it is about math!

If you think of possible combinations that you can get using items that you already have in your wardrobe, I bet you will get a pretty big number. In fact, the number you get may be so huge that you will feel you have no clue as to how you would even manage to implement all these ideas; you will not have enough days in a season, a calendar year, or even in many years, to wear all these combinations even once. What's more, when you focus on the endless possibilities your wardrobe offers, it can help curb the temptation to buy new items unnecessarily, saving both money and space. By viewing your existing wardrobe as a creative challenge, you might just discover a whole new appreciation for what you already own.

Imagine if we were as dedicated to our health and fitness as we often are to our possessions. We would be much healthier, prettier, and happier, and we would save ourselves a good amount of money as well. Imagine yourself thinking you have done squats but have not worked on your abs for a whole week, and then you can't wait to wake up to it the next day. People who do this *are* generally healthier and happier. When people work on a certain group of muscles, they do not do all possible exercises at once but select several. They know that some exercises go well together, and some do not; they will do some today and some on a different day. And as long as these exercises are enough to work on a specific group of muscles, it is all good. The same principle applies to outfits (and possessions in general): not everything goes well with everything else. As long as you create a good look (or a beautiful and cozy house, etc.), you do not need to have all of those potential possible combinations at once. Often, less is better. When you focus on quality rather than quantity, you'll find that your choices feel more intentional and satisfying. Curating your wardrobe or space in this way can reduce decision fatigue and make your daily routines much simpler and more enjoyable. Additionally, embracing the concept of "less is more" often brings a sense of peace and clarity, helping you appreciate and make the most of what you already have.

This sounds obvious, doesn't it? Now, why are we not used to matching and combining things we have in a refreshing and elegant way? This is not really our fault or necessarily a lack of sense of style. This is our culture, a culture of consumption that we live in. We are encouraged to buy more and more; we are made to believe that fashion is different every season. While, essentially, it repeats itself over and over again in different combinations. We are shown by mannequins and ads that these specific pants will only go best with this specific top or type of accessory. Nope, they do not; they go well with everything that looks good to them.

If you think these lines were written by someone who has always had and followed this logic, let me remind you where I started from—me trapped in the jungle of my own stuff in my room, not knowing how I even got there, and how I had a feeling that I did not even possess enough stylish and pretty things. It was not through this logic that I looked at things differently; the logic came later after I felt trapped and built confidence through practice. What seriously helped me was my little modeling experience. It may have been a subconscious internal cry for help, as I came to this as an excuse for my abundant wardrobe. I felt bad having numerous items of clothing and cheap jewelry and wanted to justify it. Of course, back then, I would not have admitted that, but now I know and can do so with a laugh. Something similar happens when I observe people go to a number of parties and events not because they are terribly interested in them but rather so that they can put on that fancy outfit they just obtained. Sometimes, they even partially admit that. Nothing wrong with this, but we need to realize that this leads to the fact that we choose the way we live for the sake of the things we have, while it should be the other way around. We should choose things we have for the sake of the life we want to live. When we focus on curating possessions that genuinely align with the life we envision, we start to see our choices in a new light. It's not about owning things for their own sake but about how these items serve to enrich our experiences, goals, and relationships. This mindset shift can be liberating, allowing us to declutter both physically and mentally as we align our surroundings with what truly matters.

Moreover, when we stop letting material items dictate our decisions, we open up the possibility of living more authentically. Instead of accumulating fleeting satisfaction, we can create a space for long-lasting joy—whether that comes from meaningful connections, pursuing passions, or cherishing simplicity.

So, going back to the topic, I felt bad for having a lot of things and, even worse, for not using them enough. In fact, half of the things were barely or never worn—the reason being I asked myself each time," Isn't it too fancy, bright, new, expensive, etc.?" Sometimes, I even allowed my clumsy childhood fears in: "Isn't it too good to wear it now? What if I put a stain on it or tore it?" Sure, as a kid, I would definitely go climb trees and fences, play soccer and hide-and-seek, and make that cute thing as dirty as possible and as torn as a fishing net, and in the evening, my Mom would definitely kick my ass for that and remind me that things like this should only be worn for a special occasion. Come on, seriously? Believe it or not, laugh at me or not, but it actually took me a number of years to come to the wise conclusion that if I have something, it is better to use it a lot until it cannot be used any more than to give the object eternal well-being by simply never using it. Why did I even have it, right? So, I was saying to myself that I would wear these things someday, which was not coming, and so I kept walking around in the same set of usually not-so-elegant clothing while my closet fought with me every time I tried to close the doors completely. Seriously, this is how silly it was. Over time, I realized that by not using things, I was depriving myself of the joy and confidence they could bring. The idea that something is "too good" for the present moment creates a barrier between us and enjoying life as it happens. Waiting for a "special occasion" often means those occasions never come—or when they do, we've already outgrown or forgotten the items we were saving.

Additionally, by holding onto unworn or unused items, I was unknowingly contributing to the clutter in my life—both physical and emotional. Letting go of the mindset that objects must be preserved for some future ideal allowed me to embrace what I had in the present and to use and enjoy these things fully. There's a certain satisfaction in giving your possessions a purpose and seeing them as tools to enhance your life rather than trophies to keep in pristine condition.

When the right circumstances presented themselves to do a little bit of photo modeling for some small projects and showcase clothes by small local designers, I took this opportunity as a side hobby. It all started at Starbucks when I asked a guy at the neighboring table, who turned out to be a photographer if he could watch my things when I went to the washroom. Speak about the small world. With little knowledge in this field, except that you should look good, dress well, make pretty faces, and pose in front of the camera, one thing I realized rather quickly was that I had way more very usable and lovely things than I had thought. When you need to use your wardrobe at a practice or time-for-print photoshoot, you normally bring with you a big bag or even a suitcase of different outfits, accessories, shoes, and makeup products. I remember my first several experiences – I took with me as many "fancy things" as I possibly could. And then not only myself, but also the photographers had fun choosing which of these items I should use first, second, and last. I am being sarcastic here, as this is a photographer's nightmare, to have to choose with a model her outfits again and again in a very busy and time-restricted setting. Good thing I was also helping them set up their equipment. And no, they were not asking me, but I was very curious and generally all over the place, as well as nostalgic for my previous job as an event assistant who set up rooms and equipment. So, we did get along; they liked my personality, and this added to the piggy bank of their patience with me.

Pretty soon, I learned to combine and match things rather well. Knowing my wardrobe very well, I would quickly come up with ideas in my head, pair things up, and throw just a few of them in my suitcase. I got to practice this more as an extra and photo double in movies later, as we also needed to bring a few outfits to the location that could be a good fit for your tiny role on set. It always cracked me up how we were often addressed as "background performers" when our act was very minimal, and we would barely be shown for a few seconds if that. It was a great experience – very fun, interesting, and useful as practice for quite a few things, including a sense of style and quick matching of items, makeup, etc. Not to mention, on the sidenote, all the food, we got to eat in between our effort-consuming acting episodes (yes, I am joking here).

Anyhow, since then, I have not had any difficulty choosing the right outfit (from what I have) and perfecting it (with what I have). Thank you, modeling—lesson learned. I do not even look much at all of those clothes displayed in stores behind the glass along the streets, with mannequins in weird poses. I remember staring at those displays with my eyes doubling in size and my legs forgetting where I was heading. Now, if I look at clothing and accessories, this is more to upgrade my sense of style. And if I do need something, then yes, I may buy it. But I do not feel an urge.

So, should we summarise? You do not need a large number of things in each category in order to diversify your looks. You can look differently in the same outfit if you change details, such as a belt, a scarf, a purse, shoes, hairstyle, lip color or makeup, accessories, etc.). Don't you sometimes stand in front of a mirror unable to decide which of two or three things go best with your outfit? Well, the answer is – all of them can go well. There are different possible combinations, so when you choose one, you may want to keep the other combinations in mind for the future.

## Know What You Have and Use It All

Did you know that in the U.S., sixty percent of clothing purchased each year is never worn, sitting in closets or drawers with tags still attached to them? This sounds crazy, doesn't it? But can you say with all honesty that you are using all the items you have? I cannot. Many of us use only a small part of what we have. This creates a contradiction - on the one hand, you feel like you are flooded with stuff; on the other hand, you constantly get the impression that you do not have enough. This is because we do not even remember many items we have or save them for some special mysterious occasion that never comes. Thus, we have active and passive items – ones that we use and ones we do not. This disconnect between what we have and what we use can make us feel overwhelmed as if we are accumulating things without truly benefiting from them. Often, the sense of having too much can create clutter in our lives, both physically and mentally, making it harder to focus on what truly matters.

Use all you have. If you do not use something, then find a better place for it – give it away or find another way you can use the item. This way, you will only have things that you actually use – so you won't be drowning in a sea of stuff. At the same time, you will use everything you have – so you will have everything you need. You will see a version of yourself that you like daily and in real life – not solely in your imagination – and you will feel little to no urge to buy new things. A key to using all your items is knowing them all first. Admit that if once you buy an item, you push it to the far corner of your closet and forget about it, then technically, you do not really know it. You may want to arrange all your items in a way that they are all visible and easily accessible. Once you see an item that you do not need anymore, consider letting go of it. Regularly reassess what truly adds value to your life. Sometimes, we hold onto things out of habit or sentimentality, but if an item no longer aligns with who you are or what you need, it's okay to let go. This helps you create space not only in your physical environment but also mentally and emotionally, fostering a more intentional way of living.

So, how do you make using all your items easier? Once you buy something, use it right away or as soon as possible. If it is a clothing item, put it on for a day or at least wear it in the house for fifteen minutes, so you familiarise yourself with the new item and will remember it and how it is to use it, so that when you are busy, or sleepy, or in a hurry and looking for a quick choice, the item does not get forgotten as an option. Welcome your items. You bought something – allocate time for it to 'meet and greet' your item. This will bring the item from the 'will be used one-day' category, likely to be forgotten in the back of the closet or storage, to an item already in use. Another approach is to rotate items in your wardrobe regularly, bringing those that are not often worn to the front or placing them somewhere visible. This simple step helps ensure that no item stays forgotten for too long and reminds you of all the possibilities you already have at your disposal. Also, when you actually use the items, you see that you don't lack their replacements and will be less likely to buy identical, similar items. Another benefit of this is that you will see more clearly that you are exchanging your time for this item. When you make it a rule for yourself to allocate time to meet and understand each new item upon buying/receiving it the same day or the next day, you will be more aware of the time–item exchange. You may look at unnecessary items as commitments, not just easy, pleasant rewards.

Now, if these items are clothes, I suggest you make yourself look good when you 'meet' them. The reason for this is that your opinion of the item depends on how you look at it. And for you to look good in it, a big part is for you to look good in general. If you did not brush your hair, wash your face and do what you normally do when you go out to meet your friends or to work, the item may not make the impression you were expecting. I bet when you saw it in an ad, the person wearing it looked groomed enough, did they? Don't set your items up for failure from the beginning. Give them a fair opportunity. If the item is, let's say, a set of outdoor games, go play them outside, even if just for fifteen minutes. This works with all types of items. If the situation where the item would be used is not something that happens often, pretend, act it out, even if for a little bit. Having the mental picture and memory of you using your items in real life helps you use them later. When you make an effort to truly experience and familiarize yourself with an item, you begin to appreciate its value more. It no longer feels like an abstract purchase but something that tangibly adds to your life. This can also help you become more mindful of the things you buy in the future, as you'll be less likely to accumulate items that you won't fully use or appreciate.

## Prioritise the Timeless

Now, what if the item is out of fashion? With clothes, furniture, and much more, you can say there is a timeless style and there are tons of other styles of trends that come and go or that you would only go to on very specific occasions.

I remember showcasing a new collection of clothes by a local designer at a small music and fashion event. It was a pleasant and fun experience, and I got to meet some great people. I also had a giggle or two, mostly to myself, as I tried not to show it. The first giggle I owed to the fact that the trousers I was showcasing were a falling hazard. The front and back of one leg were simply not connected on the sides, and these super long front and back pieces were just moving all over the place, almost getting under my high heels. I was walking, trying not to step on these and afraid I would fall face first on the floor. It was not helping that they put me to be the first one to walk, which increased the pressure, as for the first model to fall on her face would be another level of epic fail. One could then say the collection landed. Literally, it was a bit stressful but also very funny to me. My second giggle was due to the clothes that one of the proud designers was wearing. This lovely gentleman looked like a Christmas tree, with extremely colorful patterns and lights (yes, electric lights!) on his clothes. All these outfits were kind of cool, but I asked myself where one would wear them. To work or school? No. To run daily chores? Nope. At home or a friend's? Hell no. Maybe just at some very specifically themed parties.

Maybe my simple and humble persona does not understand much about fashion trends. And this is why I asked. As I used to work at a school with a fashion design program, I remember asking the head of the program, a great guy and a very talented fashion designer, why, on the fashion show, there are so many weird items that one would never use in real life. If my memory does not deceive me, he laughed and said that these events are not to introduce the audience to new everyday items but rather to try the waters with some trends and features that are intentionally exaggerated. If these are received rather well, then they can, to a smaller degree, be implemented in real products. Now, this does make sense. And there is nothing wrong with having some trendy items here and there. However, trends come and go. If you chase these and only these, your new items will be out of style the very next season. Sneaky industry, isn't it? Many say that fashion repeats itself. But so do many cosmic events that happen once in many years. Are you going to wait? I would just go with more timeless styles, universal ones. I remember sharp-nosed shoes being very popular when I was a university student back home. I do not see these that much now. Something more universal might be a win.

## Don't be a Dog in The Manger

Somewhere there, in your household, in the depth of your storage spaces, there may sit an item or two, or maybe more, that has been wondering why you keep it if you never use it. It has been wondering why it cannot be happy with someone else who would appreciate it, why you insist on it being yours. This might be a sign that the item has outlived its purpose in your life and it's time to let go. Often, we hold onto things because of sentimental value, guilt, or the belief that we might need it one day, but in reality, it's just taking up space and adding to the clutter. Recognizing when something no longer serves us can be a liberating experience, allowing room for new things—both physical and emotional—to enter our lives.

Bypassing these items on to someone else, whether through donation or sale, you can help them find a new purpose and make someone else's life a little better. This process not only declutters your space but also makes you feel lighter, knowing that the item is appreciated and used rather than gathering dust. Sometimes, letting go is the best way to honor the role an item once played in your life.

If you, like me, grew up at a time and in an environment where getting rid of things mostly meant throwing them away unless you gave them to someone you know, you may be used to feeling subconscious guilt if an item that could still serve its purpose was to be disposed of. Add to that an environment where getting new items was sometimes not easy, and you get a perfect storm for this situation where things are kept for as long as they can be used, one day, even if that day never comes.

Fast-forward to this day. There are so many ways to donate or sell your items. We have donation locations, thrift stores, and social media groups. If an item is good but you do not use it, it becomes so easy to give it a second life with someone who will benefit from it. A quick drop off or post online – and you have done a good thing to someone, decluttered your space, and decreased the need for consumption for both yourself and the other person. Let's not be dogs in the manger. In addition to helping others, donating or selling your unused items can also bring a sense of fulfillment and mindfulness. By consciously letting go of things, you're actively choosing to live with less but more meaningfully. It's a step toward a more intentional and sustainable lifestyle where the things you own truly align with your needs and values. In this way, you not only clear your physical space but also make room for personal growth and greater satisfaction with what you already have.

## Let Your Home Help You

On one of my sleepless nights feeding my newborn I was listening to the United Kingdom YouTube channel Absolute Documentaries about hoarders and impulsive shoppers. They used an interesting concept as an interior designer who worked as a part of a team whose goal was to help these people overcome their addictions and change their lives. It was fascinating how the process focused not just on physical space but also on addressing the emotional and psychological factors that drove these behaviors. The approach highlighted how deeply intertwined our possessions can be with our sense of self and well-being.

The idea behind the interior designer's presence on the team was that a great interior and a cozy, comfortable home help reduce the urge to shop. When the designer remade people's homes and made them look great, this achieved a few things at once – created their respect for the space, which made them not want to spoil it with clutter, made them feel comfortable, happy, and excited to live in such a lovely space, and encouraged smart financial choices. The thing with this interior design makeover was that the money was to come from the person, which meant no more purchases and selling off many existing items. Only in this case, the makeover was possible. The person's wardrobe was displayed in some large space, where they faced all their belongings and were often shocked by how many they had.

If you and I keep our items organized and displayed nicely instead of being shoved into corners and drawers, we will see how much we have. If your items are organized nicely, they will be pleasing to the eye, and you will want to use them. In turn, when you have too many things, and they are piling up, it is not easy or pleasant to look for specific items, so you avoid those piles and do not use your things, which results in you buying more items to use but then pile them as well, and the story repeats itself. Organizing not only helps you make the most of what you already own, but it also brings a sense of order and control to your space, making it feel less overwhelming and more manageable.

Let's think about a store where you got any of your things from. How do items there look? They are appealing largely because of the way they are presented and organized. Let's imagine a girl, and let's call her Melissa. Melissa had a lot of pretty things – outfits, shoes, accessories, jewelry, makeup products, and perfumes. In fact, she had so many she could barely fit these in her closets and drawers, and the items were piling one on top of another in a crowded mess. She had to organize herself better, but the thought of this felt overwhelming to her. She had enough work and stress at her job, and now that it was her day off, she wanted to relax. Melissa went to the city center to meet her friend for a coffee. The two chatted for an hour or so and agreed to see each other again soon. And now Melissa had some free time. She did not really feel like going home to her housework and other tasks that were waiting for her; and the day was nice, too. So, she had a nice small walk and then walked into a mall. Her friend looked really good today, with all her fashionable clothes and accessories, and their talks were inspiring. So, Melissa was encouraged to make herself look better and feel better – starting from… now. It was her day off after a busy week, and she did not want to think about serious matters, problems, and solutions. She wanted something big, but she wanted it now. That red dress in the window looked inspiring and fit well into her dream vision of a better self. She could easily imagine herself – slimmer, healthier, and happier-looking, with great posture and perfectly styled hair – walking confidently in that dress on a date. One day, she will go on a date, that is for sure, although she has been alone for a while. She imagined how they would walk together to a nice restaurant, where she would park her car – that would also be red – and that they would have a great time before she would have to get up the next day to her dream job – that she one day hoped to find.

All these fantasies and images crossed her mind in a matter of seconds; she felt inspired and walked into the store. She did not want to make difficult decisions or changes; it was her day off after a busy work week, and she wanted to be guided by the world towards her dreams. And she allowed the mall to guide her. It felt so right, with this lovely relaxing music, big, light, and nicely arranged space, posters with happy and beautiful models on the walls, and rows of nicely arranged and beautifully folded items, grouped by colors, styles, and purpose – a pleasure for her eye. Some items were on sale, and this magic word worked like a magnet for customers – two or three ladies were already checking out items on the same rack that she was aiming for. She let herself enjoy the moment, surrendering to the atmosphere of effortless indulgence as if the store itself was promising to take care of all the decisions for her. By the time Melissa reached that red dress, she already had five or six items in her hands that she was taking with her to a fitting room. Those five or six items would look great on her new self that she was to build.

Melissa walked into the fitting room and tried the items on, one by one. She did not get that dream look she was imagining in any of these. Because what she saw in the mirror was her current real self, with all her flaws that she still had to work on. However, this did not stop Melissa. She thought that with a little more makeup and styling, she would definitely look gorgeous. Besides, the items were on sale – it was a really good price. So, she bought them. And she also bought a couple of cheap perfumes and accessories while in line at the cashier stand. She spent a good amount of money and felt a bit of guilt mixed with excitement about her new image and new life. As she walked out of the store, the thrill of the new purchases lingered, but a tiny voice inside wondered if these items would truly make her feel any different in the long run.

When Melissa came home, she was too busy to try these on again. There was not enough available space in her closet to arrange these nicely, so she just put the items in a bag, as they were in a corner of her closet, to come back to and use happily soon – which did not happen for weeks and months after. If Melissa had cleared and reorganized her closet, she would have seen how many beautiful things she had – more than enough. She would have realized how many items she had even forgotten she had bought, exactly like those she had just obtained today. If she had organized her closet nicely, like they do in stores, folded her clothes, and arranged them by color and style, she would not have felt any better in stores than in her own home and would not have felt the need to look for that feeling outside.

Now, imagine if you walked into a store and all of the items were in a mess similar to the one you have at home. Some items would be lying on the floor or hanging from a chair, while others would be hidden in the corner or piled on top of another. Would you want to proceed with looking through those? Or would you rather get out of that place as soon as possible and get some fresh air? It's hard to feel motivated to shop in an environment like that, and chances are, you would leave with a sense of frustration, much like when we feel overwhelmed by our own cluttered spaces at home. The difference is that when you organize and present things nicely, both at home and in a store, the experience becomes enjoyable and inviting, creating a sense of possibility and excitement. And yes, you could have this same pleasant sense at home with things you already have if they are arranged well.

While bigger things are easy to see and remember by organizing them nicely, little things are easy to lose, forget, or make it uncomfortable for you to access. I suggest you place your little items and accessories on display. You can use hangers for your belts and scarves and special stands for your jewelry – similar to the ones they have in stores. There are also special organizers that you can hang on your closet door to store little items you can see and easily reach. If you do store these little things in boxes and would like to continue doing this, then choose boxes with many sections where you can separate your jewelry and items by type and color. At some point I used a transparent case with eight or nine sections where I separated my earrings by color. If I was looking for something red, I would be digging into the red section, if blue, then blue, etc. It made things much easier for me, and this way, things did not get mixed, lost, or forgotten. Later on, I switched to using jewelry boxes to display every item independently. This was for two reasons - for me to see that I have more than enough instead of jamming a whole bunch of similar items in one section and to make sure I see each item right away.

## Open That Treasure Chest

There is a joke on how you can find all kinds of random items in a lady's purse. It does not have to be a lady and does not need to be a purse - in fact, any kind of storage space, portable or not, ends up hosting many more items than you think it does. The following advice I am about to give is as much for myself as it is for you. Our spaces can quickly become filled with little things that we don't really need or use regularly, but somehow, we keep them just in case. Taking the time to regularly declutter and assess what we have can help us create more space, both physically and mentally, and ensure we're only holding onto things that truly serve us.

Empty your bags and purses when you decide to put them aside for a while or, better even, every day. What often happens when we change a purse and put one aside is that we forget about items we have in that purse – and then we buy more of the same chewing gum, lipstick, tissues, combs, and other random goodness. Heck, it even happens when we keep using the bag but do not remember what treasures are buried within its depths. I know some items necessarily travel from bag to bag, like a comb, mints, chewing gum, hand cream, lipstick, a pen, maybe business cards, etc. – let's call these daily items. You may want to pick a place close to the house entrance where you keep these items after you come back home. You may even store them in one little bag. So, come home, take this little bag out of your purse, and put it in a designated place. In the morning, or whenever you go out, take this little bag and put it in the purse you are taking. Make it your habit. Yes, there is a chance you forget the whole thing. But this chance is much smaller than the probability of you forgetting at least one of those multiple items when changing bags. And once this becomes a habit, you are good. The beauty of this system is that it also reduces mental clutter and decision fatigue, making it easier to move through your day without the stress of disorganization.

Likewise, look inside your drawers regularly. If you do not have time to clean and reorganize, at least look inside to remember what you have there. You may be surprised by some unexpected treasures you find that you had thrown in there a long time ago in the hope of dealing with them later.

## Boil That Egg Yourself

Those who watched Sex and the City or many other TV shows and movies remember those lifestyles of constant shopping and eating outside with friends. Other similar behaviors that, quite frankly, do not paint a realistic picture of the everyday life of an average person, like you and I. Film and social media often create unrealistic earning and spending expectations.

With the prices of everything going up, so do the prices of food. Yet, it is much more cost-efficient to cook than to eat out or use food delivery services. Going on Skip the Dishes, Uber Eats, or other similar platforms and ordering some sandwich, pasta, or sushi delivery may not seem like much, but these bills build up until we can't help our shocked while seeing our next bank statement. It's a reminder that small habits, when repeated, have a larger impact on our finances than we often realize, making it essential to find ways to balance convenience with mindful spending.

Apart from being a type of excessive consumption habit on its own, regularly eating out or ordering food also contributes to you over-consuming in other ways. This is because of the extra stress, sense of guilt, inability to afford more meaningful types of gratification that we would like, and, as a result, us trying to go for other little fixes here and there through consumption. It is also because once we build the habit of constantly ordering things online or regularly going out to buy things, this spreads to other items and different types of shopping, too.

You do not have to be a chef or a cooking professional to cook basic meals for yourself and your family. It helps to treat cooking as your leisure time. I watch videos or listen to podcasts or audiobooks while cooking. You can also cook with someone and socialize. Healthier home-made foods can also improve your health and apart from obvious benefits related to this, decrease your need for consumption for comfort or consolation, which we discussed above.

Moreover, cooking at home gives you the freedom to choose your ingredients, allowing you to create meals that are not only healthier but also more suited to your dietary needs and preferences. This can help you avoid the hidden sugars, preservatives, and excessive sodium often found in takeout and processed foods. By mastering a few simple recipes, you also save money over time, as eating out or relying on delivery services can add up quickly, contributing to unnecessary financial strain.

# Chapter 7. Bonus – Goats to the Rescue

## Buy a Goat – Sell a Goat.

When I was little, I heard a tale. A woman complained to a sage that her life was too busy, difficult, and problematic, and she could not feel joy. The sage advised her to buy a goat. In a bit, the woman came back to him, complaining that life had become even busier and more difficult now that she had to take care of the animal. "Now sell the goat," – the sage said. The woman did so and felt very relieved and much happier than before. Anyway, this is just a tale, and no real goat suffered in the process. The point is that no matter how busy and stressful things are for you, it can always be worse. Even when you think it cannot believe me, it can. You can have the same thing but with a broken hand or any other problem that you did not even think of. Sometimes, even thinking this way helps you appreciate what you have or the fact that there is something bad you have avoided. However, this tale can be taken as a guide to action. Well, you do not have to take it literally and have a goat farm unless you want to. Nothing against goats. Goats are adorable animals. But this tale is to say that you can always take upon something that will make your life even more difficult and then resolve it or get rid of it. The important part is recognizing that you can face challenges, no matter how tough they seem at first. Sometimes, taking on a new responsibility or challenge, even if it feels overwhelming, can teach you valuable lessons in resilience, patience, and creativity. Once you've dealt with that extra weight, you may find yourself stronger and better equipped to handle future obstacles, ultimately making your life more fulfilling and rewarding. Additionally, resolving this additional challenge will bring you a sense of joy and satisfaction and make your life without that challenge seem much easier and more pleasant. Also, the beauty of it is that you do not have to give yourself motivational speeches; as you throw this new challenge at yourself, you literally have no choice but to solve it, so you throw yourself into this problem-solving mode that is much more productive than the mode of complaining and contemplation.

## When and how does it work?

I often use this method when I feel stuck. Sometimes, things do not just go poorly; they do not even move, and I do not get any emotional reward but have to feed on frustration and stress. Then I think, well if I am already having a difficult time and am not enjoying life as much anyway, why not add a bit more to it? I will work my ass off and then relax. This goat method – let me call it this way because it is fun – helps you feel an achievement reward if you solve something extra, a relief if you take it up and then get rid of it, or/and can help get more stuff done while you are not at your best so that later, when you are, you have more freedom to enjoy things you love.

So, I would say that there are two types of goats – impactful goats and temporary goats. The latter ones are those that you take upon yourself as an extra difficulty in order to remind yourself that things could be worse, and then send these goats away and feel relief – literally what happened in the story with the woman. We will focus on the other type – impactful goats. These are ones that you do need and want in your life – things that will be useful anyway and that need to or may as well be done and that you are consciously throwing on your head at a moment when you do not have to do it, or at least not yet.

I remember having jet lag – a trip from Russia to Canada is about twenty hours, and the time difference is eleven to twelve hours. I also had the bad flu and muscle pain – too much of a workout after no workout at all, inspired by guilt for eating too much of my Ukrainian Grandma's delicious food. At the same time, I was also working intensively on my Master's thesis day and night, going through a ton of books in Chinese and English, processing and organizing information, and editing the whole thing. My logic was the following: if I am already suffering – which means I will not enjoy these days anyway, why don't I get more things done? And then, when I feel good, I will be free to enjoy some rest and do something I want to do.

Please note that this method takes the bad type of adrenaline – stress – and converts much or at least some of it into the good type of adrenaline. At first, you are stressed and troubled by something that fell on your poor head and is haunting you and getting on your nerves. You may feel physically unwell, too, and it may seem that you just downgraded to a primitive organism and are not capable of anything. You may have a bad cold, an insane workload, experiencing heartbreak, following a medical treatment, or a strict and unpleasant diet. You admit and accept the fact that you will be stuck with this for a while no matter what – your work will not get done by itself like in a fairy tale; your cold will not go away just because you asked it; and your heartbreak will not heal after an Oreo cookie or a drunk night at a club. The last example will make it worse, by the way, as you will have a bad hangover, a sense of guilt, and increased loneliness. So, this may be the time to get a goat. You may need it. Take upon yourself a goat, or even goats, if you are a hardcore individual and like challenges. Please don't overdo it, though. You do not want to feel even worse after, right? Too many goats tend to be too heavy, especially if you feed them daily.

So, you take upon a goat a challenge or task that is useful for you anyway – like getting in shape, re-organizing your stuff, learning a useful skill, making your resume look more professional and less like your biography, etc. Something that may even be interesting and can upgrade you in a way. When good times come, you will already be an upgraded version of yourself, and if this becomes your habit, you may even upgrade faster than an iPhone. Taking on a challenge during tough times not only keeps you engaged and productive but also helps shift your focus from the pain or discomfort you're experiencing. It turns a negative situation into an opportunity for personal growth, and when you finally emerge from the hardship, you'll find yourself stronger, wiser, and more resilient.

## How to Treat Your Goats

Before you welcome a goat into your life, please make sure you turn your sense of humor on. I am sure that you already know why. Because you may want some defence when making your life more difficult and because it is such a magical instrument of turning negativity into positivity. So, humor on and goat in. Taking a goat on with a very serious and tired attitude is like digging yourself a pit that you would later fall in and have to get out of—and when you fall in, the goat will also fall on your head— so do not do it. Humor acts as a shield, softening the impact of life's challenges. When you approach difficult situations with a lighthearted attitude, it allows you to navigate them more easily, reducing stress and making it easier to bounce back when things get tough. Laughter truly can be a lifesaver when you're balancing your own "goats."

Goats can become your best buddies when you are upset or feel you cannot change something and have to go through with it no matter what. You can go cry to your friend, and it may help, once, twice, but not every day for a month – and one day, you may find your friend crying in depression too, after being fed your misery like this for a month. You can pity yourself or try to get distracted in nightclubs, bars, or shopping malls, but these will most probably not solve the issue. So, what you can do is – right, get yourself a goat or a couple of them. When everything in your life seems out of control, and you feel stuck, invite into your life something that you can actually change or accomplish. You can take something that you want to work on in your life anyway. I work hard on getting in better shape, for example. It became a habit and is even funny, as once I feel overwhelmed with something, I automatically start doing squats, sit-ups, or push-ups. It came to a point where, upon waking up in the morning, I would start working on my abs while still in bed – funny but useful.

Love your goats. You were the one who welcomed them into your life. And you did this so that they could help you. Remind yourself how precious these goats are and how helpful their company is. Do not expect that the goats will solve all your problems and bring you ultimate happiness all at once – if this were the case, everyone would have been doing this all the time; there would be no depression and no drugs—only goats everywhere. You still go through whatever you have to go through. You may cry in the rain every day for a while, inspired by the songs of A-ha; you may follow a difficult and rather torturous diet or treatment or deal with some work that you find boring and annoying. These things will not go away or magically evaporate. But what *will* happen is that by the time you are done with these, you will have also resolved more things in your life (goats), upgraded yourself, and brought yourself to a better you and a better reality. And, in the process, you will have had emotional rewards through challenges and achievements—all with a sense of humor. And when, after all that crying in the rain, you are out in the sun again, you are a new, upgraded person, ready and excited for a new present and future. This goat method keeps you occupied, balances the effort-reward relationship, and turns stress into positive adrenaline.

# Part III. Smart Exchange

---

## Chapter 1. Our Resources and Choices

In the previous sections of the book, we have talked about a number of psychological triggers and some neuroscience and technical tricks; let us look at this matter from one more perspective – from the perspective of constant resource exchange on various levels. In fact, we have already touched upon this, but in this part of the book I would like to focus on this aspect specifically. The way we allocate our time, attention, and energy ultimately shapes our outcomes. It's crucial to understand how our resources are distributed across various areas of life—whether that be our personal goals, work, relationships, or even our possessions. This conscious awareness can allow us to optimize our investments for the best possible returns in terms of well-being, fulfillment, and growth.

When you think of the word 'resources' in relation to an individual, what comes to mind? In a society obsessed with consumption and materialism, the first things that come to many minds are financial and material resources – the amount of money they have in their bank account, their property, and assets. Then, if you think more, there come such things as time, physical resources (health), and intellectual resources (your intelligence, experience, and education).

I entered the word 'resources' into a Google search, and almost everything that came up on the first page had to do with money, finances, and material things. I also saw land, labor, capital, energy, information, expertise, and time. All of these have to do with an organization or individual being able to function and be useful. A company uses its financial and human resources in order to operate. Individuals classified as human resources use their time, labor, energy, and expertise in order to perform their functions within the company. These resources are exchanged for financial resources (salary, bonuses, etc.), and all these types of resources are important and interconnected. Inevitably, we have become used to viewing things as resources and also viewing ourselves as resources, therefore materializing and objectifying ourselves. We evaluate what we can offer to the outside world and what we can get from the outside world in exchange. This sounds logical and clear, and this is how the world runs, but we miss an important point: what do we want to do in life, and what do we want to be? I do not mean your profession, your income, your apartment, or your car; I mean your personality and things that you would like to *experience and live.*

Everything we do is a sort of resource exchange. On an individual level, we exchange time, health, and energy for things we do (activities) or money, material goods, etc.

We all have a limited amount of time, energy, and health. And while it is possible to borrow some money if we need to do so, no one in this world will ever be able to lend you an extra minute of your life or transfer to your account an amount of your energy or health. It seems like an obvious fact. However, people still manage to underestimate the resources that are most valuable and irreplaceable. If everything we do is an exchange, then it makes sense we exchange resources wisely, so that the exchange brings us joy and improvement. So, if we exchange our time and energy on an activity, we better love that activity; it better be meaningful, helpful, and so on. And if we exchange these for money, we better exchange the money we get for something that is of real value to us. From this point of view, excessive consumption of things we do not really need sounds like a waste. It is not just a waste of your money BUT also a waste of your time, which is a wasted memory in this life. Moreover, the time and energy you spend on chasing fleeting trends or material possessions could be better spent on enriching experiences, learning new things, or nurturing relationships. It is essential to consider whether what you are investing in will truly contribute to your long-term well-being or if it's simply a momentary distraction.

This realization doesn't just apply to buying things but extends to how we spend our days, our effort, and our emotional resources. Are we investing them in personal growth, meaningful projects, or self-care, or are we overcommitting to activities and obligations that drain us without offering any true benefit?

## Would You Rather?

*"Nowadays people know the price of everything and the value of nothing."*

*– Portrait of Dorian Grey, by Oscar Wild.*

In interviews by various networks that you can find on YouTube, some shopaholics said that shopping was their hobby. "What else would I do with my time," they would ask. Filling up their time with shopping, they did not have time to develop hobbies and therefore, did not have hobbies to fill their time with instead of shopping. A cursed loop. A lot of time that will never come back and that does not have any memories to offer other than those of constant shopping. This pattern of consumption, fuelled by the need to fill an emotional void or boredom, prevents them from exploring other passions or interests that could bring deeper satisfaction.

One of things that help is what I call a 'would you rather' exercise. For expensive things you do not really need, imagine what else you could do and experience for this amount instead – amount of money and time. If you have hobbies, it is easy – imagine how you could dedicate more of you and your resources to these. Consider how the time spent on impulsive shopping could be better spent by learning something new, like picking up a musical instrument, practicing a new language, or even exploring a new sport. If you happen to be at a loss as for what else you would do with your time, think of something rather universal that everyone tends to enjoy – be it a small trip somewhere that you would need to save some money for, a house party that you would invite your friends to, a massage, or something else. The key here is that this experience in addition to being pleasant should also upgrade you in some way, or at least not downgrade you and not add to impulsive consumption. Think about how an experience like a trip or a massage would enhance not just your mood, but also your personal growth or sense of relaxation, giving you more value than the temporary thrill of an unnecessary purchase. For example, a massage would help reduce your stress and contribute to your general well-being; a trip would bring you new experiences and knowledge, get you out of the regular loop of things and bring excitement and memories for the future; so would a house party with your friends. If you would like to take it one step further, you may want to consider learning new skills, reading books, working out or otherwise developing yourself further intellectually or physically.

## Making the Right Choices for the Moment

People say that when we are young, we have energy and time, but do not have money; when we get older, we have energy and money, but do not have time; and as we grow old, we do have time and money, but do not have energy. Time is rather straightforward. Energy is health and mood, and money summarizes and symbolizes all the material goods in our lives. If we look deeper into this, money is just the most common example of what we can call means of achievement of what we want. I would also include in this category such things as skills, required supplies, or completion of all kind of pre-requisites needed for our goal. This is why the real wealth in our lives isn't just money or possessions, but the combination of all these elements—time, energy, and the means to achieve what we desire—working together in harmony to create a life well-lived.

While we cannot have it all at the same time, we can definitely have the best possible for us. The trick is to be able to distribute our resources wisely and to place the right focus at the right time. When we do not get the balance, we feel that something is missing, and then we may be tempted to go look for more rewards outside, which can be another dress, another can of beer, another iPhone, etc.

I often do a lot of boring and necessary work when I am not feeling well. My logic is that as I am not feeling well at the moment, I will not be able to enjoy the moment anyway, so why don't I clean the mess or do a project that I have been procrastinating on for a while? This way, I will have free time for when I do feel good enough for something more interesting or meaningful. I basically do not use the resource of free time at moments when I cannot enjoy it. I use the resource of free time when I have the energy, and perhaps, means of achieving what I want. Interestingly, I also start feeling better faster when I get distracted and do something rather than focus on my headache or another problem. This approach allows me to turn what could be an unproductive and frustrating time into an opportunity to get things done, and the sense of accomplishment can actually help lift my mood faster than just waiting for the discomfort to pass.

A similar principle can apply to a lot of things and situations. If the day outside is sunny and extremely nice, you would probably agree that it may make more sense to go for a hike with friends than to go shop for some new furniture. If you feel like you do not have energy for a hike or another sport activity, but you have a clear mind and inspiration to write something, it will most probably be better to write than to force yourself to exercise. You can do much better at exercising later when you do have a better energy for it.

The general suggestion is to go with what you can do most efficiently at the moment. When you do have a choice, of course. You will be much more productive and happier, as you will be doing what you want at the moment and following your intuition. This approach not only helps you avoid unnecessary stress but also allows you to align your actions with your current energy levels, mindset, and capabilities. When you work with the flow of the moment, you can achieve tasks with greater ease and satisfaction, ultimately improving both your well-being and productivity.

When you look back on everything we have discussed so far and add this new angle to it, look at it through the prism of a smart exchange.

## Thinking Flexibly - Freedom of Movement

This one is a simple point. The less you have, the easier it is for you to move around and change your life, to start a new chapter and to have fewer concerns and matters to take care of should there come a change in your life. By embracing a more minimalistic lifestyle, you create more space, both physically and mentally, which allows you to adapt to new opportunities or challenges with greater ease. You are not weighed down by things that are unnecessary or no longer serve your purpose, making your journey smoother and more focused. Remember, there is a ninety-nine percent chance that all the stores are not closing tomorrow, and therefore, you should be able to purchase what you need when you need it. Do not put this extra burden on yourself now when you do not need the item. This approach frees up your time, energy, and resources, allowing you to focus on things that truly matter to you and your future goals. In this ever-changing world with all kinds of challenges coming your way, flexibility is important.

It is good to remember that the less you buy, the more financial resources you save. This saved money can be invested in experiences or opportunities that enhance your well-being or personal growth rather than spent on material possessions that may only offer temporary satisfaction. This also gives you more freedom and flexibility. With fewer financial commitments tied to unnecessary purchases, you have more control over your future decisions and can allocate your resources towards long-term goals, whether that be travel, education, or building a secure future.

And last but not least—time. The more resources you have available to you, the less time you have to spend surviving and making ends meet. This allows you to focus on personal growth, creative pursuits, and building meaningful relationships instead of constantly worrying about immediate survival needs. Thus, you have more time and freedom to use it the way you please. With greater stability, you can prioritize what truly matters, whether it's investing in your health, expanding your knowledge, or simply enjoying the present moment without the pressure of constant demands.

# Chapter 2. We Take Away from Our Future

Alexander McCall Smith is a British writer who was born in Zimbabwe, spent much of his life in Africa, and wrote about it. One of his books is a collection of folk tales from Africa called "The Girl Who Married a Lion and Other Tales from Africa." In the tale "Head Tree," a tree starts growing out of a man's head. The man went to see a wise woman who claimed he had done or was planning to do something bad. She gave him a herb to take for a week and named the price for the treatment as two cows that the man promised to pay upon his recovery. When the man got rid of the tree, however, he did not pay to the woman and bit up the boy she sent to him for the payment. Then, a bigger tree started growing on his head, which left him with no option but to go back to the charming woman and bring the two cows with him. At this point, though, the disappointed woman demanded four cows from him. Thus, because of not paying before and deceiving the woman, the man had to pay the double.

We often promise ourselves to pay for certain things and behaviors ("I will eat healthy next week after going nuts this week," etc.) and do not keep our promises. We borrow from ourselves but do not return the loan. This habit creates a cycle where we feel guilty and disappointed in ourselves, which can make it even harder to take positive steps forward. Over time, these unkept promises pile up, and the weight of unfinished commitments starts to affect our confidence and motivation. Then not only do we need to pay double (go on a stricter or longer diet, for example, or save money more strictly to repay our debts), but also, we also have to restore the trust and respect we have for ourselves. When we do not do what we should at the moment, we need to understand that we borrow or take away from our future.

# Chapter 3. Life In Plastic – Not Fantastic

In addition to everything we talked about in relation to you, we should also consider common resources we share on this planet with other people and creatures, animals, and plants. These shared resources often get left out and ignored by people. Now, before you roll your eyes and say that on an individual level, we affect the planet thousands of times less than corporations, plants, and other entities, believe me, I know. It is indeed so. And in this lies a tragedy of it (as we cannot on an individual level change much), but also some relief. Relief as it takes lots of pressure off you and me while still leaving a space for us to make wise decisions. We do not need to beat ourselves up for each Amazon delivery and each plastic bag. However, when we do not really need an item, we can remind ourselves that another plastic package with stuff does not just cost you twenty dollars. It costs you an hour of the time that you spent working, time that you spent ordering and receiving it, and costs the planet some more pollution. It also means that some natural resources and a small share of human and animal species' well-being were exchanged for this piece of plastic. Do you sincerely believe that it was a smart exchange?

I bet we've all heard of the Great Pacific Garbage Patch. The scale of this thing is terrifying. It's a reminder of how deeply connected we all are to the choices made around the world. Even if you personally never litter, you're still indirectly affected by these global issues. That's why it can feel overwhelming to know where to even begin. Of course, it would be rather incorrect and even hypocritical to judge local individuals for getting some extra items. At the same time, huge corporations all over the world pollute the planet at rates you would not want to even imagine, and certain groups of individuals have absolutely different standards applied to them than the rest of the world. Not only would it not be fair, but it would also, in my opinion, not be smart or productive and would indeed have the opposite effect. Why? Because feeling this immense pressure and personal responsibility, combined with the sense of helplessness in the face of the overall scale of the matter and related hypocrisy, would contribute to one's distress and – you guessed it – impulsive behaviors.

That being said, a small change still counts as a change. Each small step you take is like planting a seed that could grow into something bigger over time. Even choosing reusable items over single-use ones or buying things with less packaging makes a difference. It might not solve the world's problems overnight, but it sets a positive example for others to follow. So, while I do not believe that individuals should be obsessing over minimizing their possessions everywhere, they can - again, this would not even do anything while the big issues all over the world stay unresolved — it helps to keep in mind you are living a responsible life and treating the environment with respect and accountability. In the end, everything is related, and, if anything, having fewer things and especially having less of a consume-dispose mindset adds to the good and takes away from the bad side of things. Our actions add up in small but meaningful ways. Even a simple habit, like reusing items or reducing waste, contributes to a bigger collective effort. When multiplied by millions of people, these choices can start to shift patterns over time. And perhaps just as importantly, they shape our mindset toward being more thoughtful and aware.

If you, like me, think that the amount of plastic packaging on everything these days is crazy, you may want to consider opting out of it whenever it makes sense. When I buy something at a store, for example, and see how they are about to wrap the living hell out of the item, I often ask them not to do so if it is not necessary. This is a tiny thing in the scale of the world, but this is a tiny good thing instead of a tiny bad one and it literally requires no effort or resources from me. Besides, it leads to a smaller amount of clutter at home, which feels more pleasant and means less cleaning work for me in the future. Over time, these small habits can save a surprising amount of waste from ending up in landfills. You could also bring your bag or container when shopping, which helps avoid unnecessary plastic. It's also a good idea to support stores that use less packaging or offer eco-friendly alternatives. Small choices like these can encourage businesses to adopt better practices. Additionally, you can also reuse things, on which you can find a lot of valuable and creative tips all over the internet. There is a DIY (do-it-yourself) option for creative people, that can also provide for a fun activity for a get-together or your evenings with kids.

I am not trying to go crazy here and discourage everyone from any kind of consumption of plastic. I do not deem this reasonable or fair. However, in my opinion, we should stop taking things for granted as if they magically appeared for us with no consequences to ourselves, others, or the planet and adopt more of a mindset where we understand that everything comes from and at the expense of something else; everything is part of an exchange. Once we do so, we can't help but automatically become more responsible with our consumption without even thinking too much about it.

# Chapter 4. Tragic Price of Cheap Merchandise

One would have to live under a rock not to have heard of the terrible work and life conditions of those who make quick fashion items and other cheap products come into existence and be as cheap as they are. Open any search engine, and you can find hundreds of texts and videos on the topic. The stories are heartbreaking and often leave you questioning how these practices are still allowed to exist. Many workers endure long hours with little to no breaks just to make enough to survive. Even worse, they often have no voice or power to demand better treatment. From child labor to slavery and concentration camp prisoner labor, from unbelievably low pay to extremely dangerous working conditions, - all of these are inevitable products of human and corporate greed. And as if this was not enough, these workers are not the only ones who suffer; the environmental cost of producing these items so cheaply is massive. Factories that prioritize cost over ethics often dump waste into rivers and pollute the air.

The scale of disregard for human life and well-being, as well as for the wildlife and environment, is difficult to quickly and completely walk away from due to many factors, including market competition, where most try to go for the cheapest prices possible in order to be competitive. Don't we all look for cheaper products? Isn't this how we select things on Amazon? Of course, we look for quality too, but if we see two or three very similar products, we usually buy the cheaper one, don't we?

Now, I am not trying to make everyone feel bad and persuade you to buy expensive things. I am just high-level describing how this works. The reality is more complicated than just buying cheap or expensive. Many consumers want to make ethical choices, but it's hard to know the truth behind the production process. Companies often hide details about where and how their items are made, making it difficult to make informed decisions. If you are a company trying to compete with other companies, you cannot let your products be much more costly than those of your competitors. Unless you provide some exceptional value that people are willing to pay double for. Unfortunately, even when consumers pay higher prices for products, there is still no guarantee that the cost of production of these items is not very small, working conditions of the people making them not being terrible, and the company not making a huge buck by making you believe otherwise and keeping the difference. Heck, many expensive fashion brands have their items production outsourced in ways far from ideal. This is why transparency in the production process is so important, though unfortunately, not many companies are willing to provide it.

Animals also pay the price as their natural habitats get affected or as their fur or skin is used in manufacturing. When it is not necessary for our survival, I believe it is much better to go for options that do not involve potential animal cruelty. As for the animals' habitats and the flora and fauna in general, industrial waste and the aforementioned plastic pose a danger to their natural state.

Thankfully, facts are coming out and people around the world do put a certain pressure on companies for ethical manufacturing. More campaigns and movements are raising awareness about where products come from and how they're made. Social media has also become a tool for exposing unethical practices and calling for better standards. However, the same people still buy items that were not produced in a way that they advocate for. And how could one judge if we often do not know and if, in the current economy, most of us barely make ends meet? We simply cannot afford to pay triple for everyday things. It is about survival and practicality for many. Ethical choices are often more expensive, and not everyone has the luxury to prioritize them over basic needs. I do not have an easy answer to the question of how to solve these problems. But I believe that thinking in this direction is already a big thing that can lead to those little things that can slowly but surely contribute to a change.

So, what can we do if we are not all walking money bags and are also not ready for a minimalist lifestyle? One approach could be to focus on buying less but choosing better. This means taking time to research and invest in items that truly meet your needs and will last. It's not about spending a fortune but about spending wisely. I remember my surprise when I realized that the total amount of money I had spent on cheap, low-quality items of all types that did not last long and needed replacement was bigger than what I would have spent on a couple of items of the kind that would be of high quality and would last much longer. Damn, those pairs of cheap shoes I got from Shein and other such sites that did not even fit nicely (what a surprise, considering the fact that I could not try them on) or were just not good cost me more in total than two-three pairs of higher quality shoes that I have now been using for years and absolutely love. Not only did I waste money, but I also wasted time dealing with returns or trying to make those items work. And let's not forget the environmental impact of producing and disposing of all these short-lived items. The majority of those cheap shoes ended up not being used by me at all. So, how did this money-saving through quick fashion go for me? Not so fantastic.

By no means am I trying to tell people what to do? In fact, I am also trying to figure it out myself and have no clear idea of a perfect solution if such exists. But thinking along these lines and keeping these ideas in mind is helpful, and each can find a good balance that would contribute to a better, smarter exchange of resources for you and others.

# Chapter 5. The Choice is Yours to Make

Money is not a primary concept. It is a derivative, a secondary concept, an intermediary between time, effort, skill, usefulness, or any other kind of primary resource. At its core, money is just a representation of value, and how much we value something often depends on what we are willing to trade for it. It is a tool for measuring unmeasurable and incomparable categories. This tool helps transfer time and labor into the amount of food we can get, land and places available to us, etc. In a way, money allows us to quantify things that are not easily measured, such as the worth of our time or the value of our experiences. And it is you and only you who decide for yourself what categories and resources you are willing to exchange for what. Each person sets their limits, deciding what is worth more to them at any given moment. For example, you may decide that your personality is not exchangeable for money and that you can perform your functions as an employee but are not willing to act against your values, beliefs, or preferences in exchange for financial resources. This is a clear example of how our choices reflect what we truly prioritize in life. A similar thing happens when we reject an offer to work on a statutory holiday for double the pay because we decide that our time with family, friends, or an interesting project is more important to us than the pay. We constantly make choices without even acknowledging it; we choose from a number of different resources and decide to make certain exchanges.

*Exercise:*

*Try to be conscious of your actions and purchases in the sense that you are aware of the fact that you are making a certain exchange. When getting an item you are not sure you really need, think of the following:*

- *How much it costs, and how much time you worked in order to get this amount? Think what you could spend that amount of money on. Maybe your favorite hobby or a good time with people you care about.*

- *Think what else you could buy for the same amount that would bring more joy to you or another person and would have a bigger positive impact in the short or long term.*

- *Think of the shared resources of the planet exchanged for this item. Are you sure you would like to promote this type of exchange further?*

*See if you consider this a good and smart exchange.*

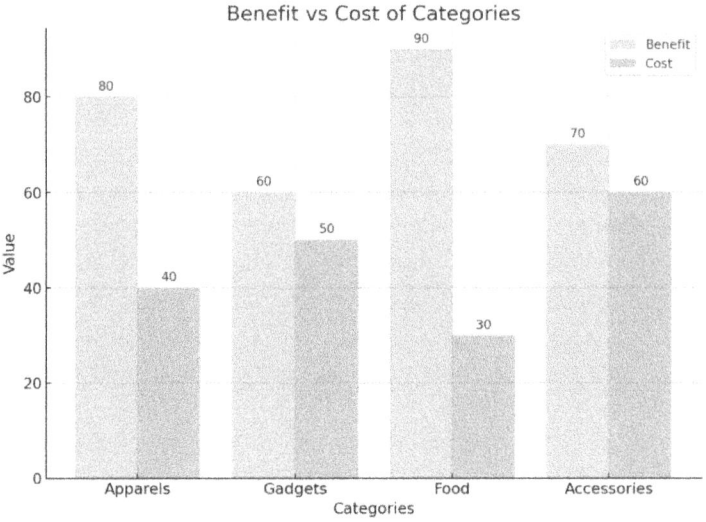

Fig. 4. Example of Approximate Benefit Vs Cost Comparison

# Chapter 6. Consumerism: How Far Has It Gone?

*"Nowadays people know the price of everything and the value of nothing,"*

*Oscar Wilde, The Picture of Dorian Gray.*

The problem of excessive consumption is a worldwide one and one you should not underestimate. Not only on a collective level but also on an individual level, it leads to financial strain, mental and physical health decline, decreased happiness, and addiction. It can also affect our relationships with others. Globally, excessive consumerism threatens the environment and deepens social inequality, and consequently, we have unsustainable practices and waste accumulation. One of the core impacts of overconsumption is a defect in global connections that directly breeds loneliness on a massive scale. Now, you will be wondering how loneliness is. Well, if the material consumes us, it takes away our focus, time, and energy from relationships with others. It also shifts our values and priorities. Additionally, especially with social media, the divide between people who seem to have it all and show it off and those who barely make ends meet is more obvious than ever. Unrealistic expectations, feelings of failure, and hopelessness are among the things that inevitably come out of this.

So, how far has it all gone? Estimates suggest that around 5-8% of the world's population suffers from compulsive shopping disorder; if I got the numbers right, there are estimated to be between 2 and 3 million people with shopping problems in Canada, around 8 million people in the UK and between 6.5 million to 52 million in the United States. It is a very large share of the total world's population; we need to be careful. But I think we are not paying the due attention.

Compulsive shoppers can accumulate debt averaging between $10,000 to $15,000, significantly impacting their financial stability. Over 60% of shopping addicts report symptoms of anxiety and depression, with many using shopping as a coping mechanism.

Now, let's talk about the wastage. The numbers are insane, and the quantity is unsurmountable. About 1.3 billion tons of food, or one-third of the total food produced, is wasted each year globally. It means that for every out of 10 hotdogs purchased, three are wasted. Due to overconsumption, we humans are losing sight of gratitude because of this, we are pushed to have weak mental conditions. We just want more and more; nobody is being grateful for what they already have. It is becoming a societal disaster, and we anymore are paying a great price for it – on both individual and global levels.

After food, there is plastic that is produced more than anything in the world. Over 300 million tons of plastic are produced annually, with only 9% being recycled. Where is the remaining mountain going? Well, not to hell, but definitely to bring this world closer to a living hell, for example, for animals that fall victim to irresponsibly discarded waste items. I am sure you have seen all kinds of sad pictures. Plastic is burnt across different countries, contributing to most of the world's pollution contributing to such 'pleasantries' as acid rains and more.

The global fashion industry generates over 92 million tons of waste each year, with consumers buying 60% more clothing than in the year 2000. Do we need more clothes now than before? No! We need the same amount, but our excessive consumption is now heading to a peak. Today, we are buying more than we need or even more than we want to; it is out of our hands now, especially in the case of fashion.

Today, a large chunk of our communication and entertainment relies on phones, tablets, and laptops. But less do we know how much of appliances are being made just to go trash and never to be recycled again. Approximately 50 million tons of e-waste are generated globally each year, with only 20% being recycled properly. The rest is either burnt or dumped in the sea, causing horrific damage to marine life.

Now, most of us are not addicts. But I bet most of us do have space for improvement when it comes to the problem of overconsumption. In fact, it is better to work on self-improvement in this field earlier rather than later because the deeper one is into something, the more reluctant they are to admit it, and the more pressure one feels and the more fixes one needs.

# Short Conclusion

We have come to the end of this book. There is still so much more to be said on this topic, and I have been tempted to include more and dig into a whole additional ocean of resources and information. But, like with consumption, it is important to know when to stop. If the topic and concepts included in this book resonated with you, you can find much more of different useful information and insight all over the internet. Among many others, I suggest the following search keywords and phrases: 'consumerism,' 'consumerism resistance,' 'impulsive consumption,' 'dopamine,' 'dopamine addiction,' 'dopamine detox,' 'mindful consumerism,' 'impulse buying psychology,' 'psychological triggers of consumerism,' 'limbic system,' 'trauma and clutter,' etc.

I hope you found this book helpful and I would like to thank you for reading it or listening to it and diving with me into the topic of consumerism resistance. Have a wonderful day!